LYNN NOTTAGE

Lynn Nottage has been awarded the Pulitzer Prize for Drama twice (for *Sweat* and *Ruined*), the first woman ever to do so. Her plays have been produced in the US and throughout the world, including *Sweat* (Pulitzer Prize, Susan Smith Blackburn Prize, Evening Standard Award, Olivier Award nomination; Donmar Warehouse, West End); *Ruined* (Pulitzer Prize, Obie Award, the New York Drama Critics' Circle Award, the longlist Evening Standard Award, the shortlist South Bank Sky Arts Award, Susan Smith Blackburn Prize finalist; Almeida); *Intimate Apparel* (the American Theatre Critics Award, New York Drama Critics' Circle Awards, the shortlist Evening Standard Award, Susan Smith Blackburn Prize finalist; Theatre Royal, Bath and Park Theatre); *Fabulation, or the Re-Education of Undine* (Obie Award; Tricycle Theatre); *The Odds* (as part of *Decade*; Headlong). Her other work includes *Mlima's Tale*, *Intimate Apparel* (the opera, composed by Ricky Ian Gordon), *Crumbs from the Table of Joy*, *By the Way, Meet Vera Stark*, *Las Meninas*, *Mud, River, Stone*, *Por'knockers*, *POOF* and *The Secret Life of Bees* (musical, lyrics by Susan Birkenhead and music by Duncan Sheik).

Nottage is the co-founder of the production company Market Road Films. She was a writer/producer on the Netflix series *She's Gotta Have It*, directed by Spike Lee, and Consulting Producer on Apple TV's series, *Dickinson*.

Nottage is the recipient of a number of distinctions including, PEN/Laura Pels Master American Dramatist Award; an Award of Merit Medal and a Literature Award from the Academy of Arts and Letters; a Doris Duke Artist Award; a MacArthur 'Genius Grant' Fellowship; a Steinberg Distinguished Playwright Award: a Nelson A. Rockefeller Award for Creativity; the Dramatists Guild Hull-Warriner Award; the inaugural Horton Foote Prize; Guggenheim Grant and NBT's

August Wilson Playwriting Award. She is an Associate Professor at the Columbia School of the Arts, and is member of the Dramatists Guild, WGAE, the American Academy of Arts and Letters and is currently an artists-in-residence at the Park Avenue Armory.

Lynn Nottage

CRUMBS FROM THE TABLE OF JOY

NICK HERN BOOKS
London
www.nickhernbooks.co.uk

A Nick Hern Book

Crumbs from the Table of Joy first published in Great Britain in 2021 as a paperback original by Nick Hern Books Limited, The Glasshouse, 49a Goldhawk Road, London W12 8QP, by special arrangement with Theatre Communications Group, Inc., New York

Crumbs from the Table of Joy copyright © 2004, 2021 Lynn Nottage

Lynn Nottage has asserted her moral right to be identified as the author of this work

Cover image: iStock.com/Igor Alecsander

Designed and typeset by Nick Hern Books, London
Printed in the UK by Mimeo Ltd, Huntingdon, Cambridgeshire PE29 6XX

A CIP catalogue record for this book is available from the British Library

ISBN 978 1 83904 002 3

Crumbs from the Table of Joy received its world premiere at
Second Stage Theatre in New York City (Carole Rothman,
Artistic Director; Suzanne Schwartz Davidson, Producing
Director), in May 1995. The cast was as follows:

ERNESTINE CRUMP   Kisha Howard
ERMINA CRUMP   Nicole Leach
GODFREY CRUMP   Daryl Edwards
LILY ANN GREEN   Ella Joyce
GERTE SCHULTE   Stephanie Roth

Director   Joe Morton
Set Designer   Myung Hee Cho
Lighting Designer   Donald Holder
Sound Designer   Mark Bennett
Costume Designer   Karen Perry
Dramaturg   Erin Sanders
Production Stage Manager   Delicia Turner
Stage Manager   David Sugarman

Crumbs from the Table of Joy received its West Coast premiere
at South Coast Repertory in Costa Mesa, California (David
Emmes, Producing Artistic Director; Martin Benson, Artistic
Director), on 17 September 1996. The cast was as follows:

ERNESTINE CRUMP   Karen Malina White
ERMINA CRUMP   Susan Patterson
GODFREY CRUMP   Dorian Harewood
LILY ANN GREEN   Ella Joyce
GERTE SCHULTE   Nancy Harewood

Director   Seret Scott
Set Designer   Michael Vaughn Sims
Lighting Designer   Paulie Jenkins
Sound Designer   Garth Hemphill

Costume Designer	Susan Denison Geller
Vocal/Dialect Consultant	Lynn Watson
Dramaturg	Jerry Patch
Production Manager	Michael Mora
Stage Manager	Randall K. Lum

Sometimes a crumb falls from the table of joy,
Sometimes a bone is flung.
To some people love is given,
To others only heaven.

Langston Hughes, 'Luck'

Characters

ERNESTINE CRUMP, *African-American, seventeen*
ERMINA CRUMP, *African-American, fifteen*
GODFREY CRUMP, *African-American, Ernestine and
    Ermina's father, thirty-five*
LILY ANN GREEN, *African-American, Ernestine and
    Ermina's aunt, thirty-five*
GERTE SCHULTE, *German, Caucasian, thirty*

Time

1950–51

Place

Brooklyn, New York City

Prologue

Fall

1950. ERMINA, ERNESTINE *and* GODFREY CRUMP *sit on a bench with their heads slightly bowed.* ERNESTINE *is a slightly plump seventeen-year-old. She wears her hair pulled tight into tiny mismatched pigtails. Her diction is crisp from practice and has the gentle inflections learned from her favorite screen actresses.* GODFREY, *a lean, handsome thirty-five-year-old man, wears an impeccably pressed suit. His appearance is always neat and well assembled.* ERMINA *is an attractive, slim fifteen-year-old; she also wears her hair in mismatched pigtails.*

ERNESTINE (*to audience*). Death nearly crippled my father, slipping beneath the soles of his feet and taking away his ability to walk at will. Death made him wail like a god-awful banshee.

GODFREY *wails like a god-awful banshee.*

Like the 12:01 steamboat mooring.

GODFREY *continues to wail.*

Death made strangers take hold of our hands and recount endless stories of Mommy. In church, at work, strolling, laughing, eating and of course at that infamous picnic in the park where half the town fell ill to Cyrinthia Bowers's potato salad.

They all laugh and shake their heads.

Death made us nauseous with regret. It clipped Daddy's tongue and put his temper to rest. Made folks shuffle and bow their heads. But it wouldn't leave us be, tugging at our stomachs and our throats. And then one day it stopped and we took the train north to New York City.

The family stands in unison. ERMINA *stands with her arms folded and her lips pursed in disgust.*

Death brought us to Brooklyn, the Nostrand Avenue stop on the A line… A basement apartment, kind of romantic, like a Parisian artist's flat.

ERMINA. If Parisian mean ugly.

ERNESTINE. Daddy worked the late shift at a bakery downtown. He'd leave every night two hours after dinner, tip his hat to Father Divine and return the next morning as we'd rise to go to school.

GODFREY *tips his hat and walks slowly, as if making his way to work. The girls walk the Brooklyn streets.*

And then we'd walk exactly fourteen blocks to school… Always thought of myself as being smart. Down home, smart meant you got homework done in time. Not so smart in… Brooklyn. They put Ermina back one grade.

ERMINA. So? (*Shrugs her shoulders and sticks out her buttocks defiantly.*)

ERNESTINE. They… them… the gals laughed at us the first day at school, with our country braids and simple dresses my mommy had sewn.

The sound of girls' laughter surrounds ERNESTINE *and* ERMINA. ERMINA *rolls her eyes.*

ERMINA. Least they clean, which is more than I can say for your tired bag of rags.

ERNESTINE (*to audience*). Our dresses were sewn with love, each stitch. But them, they couldn't appreciate it!

The laughter grows. ERMINA *prepares herself for a fight. She slicks back her hair and hitches up her dress around her thighs.*

So Ermina fought like a wild animal.

ERMINA *swings wildly in the air.*

Scratched and tore at their cashmere cardigans and matching skirts. She walked home with a handful of greasy relaxed hair and a piece of gray cashmere stuffed in her pocket.

ERMINA *basks in triumph*. ERNESTINE *strolls the streets of Brooklyn*.

Brooklyn... everything you'd ever need not more than a few blocks away. Streets of jagged slate, pennies stuck in the crevices; I collected over ten cents one day. Still, it wasn't any place to live...

She sits down. She is swathed in the brilliant, blue flickering light from a motion-picture projector.

...until I sat in the cinema, The Fox, right smack between two white gals. Oh yes! (*Looks from side to side*.) Practically touching shoulders. And we all wept. Wept unabashedly.

ERMINA *joins* ERNESTINE. *They take each other's hands*.

Watching our beautiful and wretched Joan Crawford's eyebrows and lips battle their way through one hundred and three minutes of pure unadulterated drama, we could be tragic in Brooklyn.

ERNESTINE *and* ERMINA *weep softly. The sound of the projector rolling gives way to a distant radio*.

RADIO BROADCASTER (*offstage*). Today Senator McCarthy began –

In the distance the radio dial is switched and 'Some Enchanted Evening' plays. It continues to play softly throughout the duration of the scene.

Lights rise on a sparsely decorated living room punctuated with an old standing radio/phonograph. On the mantle is a photograph of Sandra Crump, ERNESTINE *and* ERMINA*'s mother, smiling gloriously. Over the mantle hangs a huge photograph of Father Divine, the charismatic leader of the waning Peace Mission Movement, in his prime.* GODFREY *sits in an armchair reading the daily newspaper with a*

*magnifying glass, chuckling. The music from another
apartment is barely audible, taunting the girls with possibility.*

ERMINA. Now? Well?

ERMINA *awaits a response.* GODFREY *doesn't bother to
look up from his newspaper.*

GODFREY. Ain't listening!

ERMINA *walks tentatively over to the radio and flicks it on.
She shoots a quick, wide-eyed glance at* GODFREY. *Radio
laughter fills the room.*

Off!

ERMINA. Ah!

ERMINA *flips off the radio. Silence, except the distant music
of 'Some Enchanted Evening'.*

GODFREY. It's Sunday, gal!

ERMINA*'s leg shakes wildly, a nervous tic that is triggered
when she becomes agitated.* GODFREY *still doesn't look up.*

Leg's gonna fall off.

ERNESTINE (*to audience*). Almost did, but that comes later.

ERMINA (*ventures*). Ain't no use in having a radio. Might as
well be a log, 'least we could burn it to keep warm.

GODFREY. You sassing.

ERMINA. Nah, sir!

GODFREY. Could have sworn you was.

ERMINA. Really? Well, I ain't.

ERNESTINE (*to audience*). Tomorrow we'll have nothing to
talk about in school. Again, we will miss *Amos 'n' Andy.*

ERMINA. Again ruined by Father Divine. (*Rolls her eyes and
turns toward the portrait of Father Divine hanging over the
mantle.*)

ERNESTINE (*whispered, to audience*). Father Divine... Ever since Mommy passed on, he stands between us and our enjoyment. Daddy discovered Father Divine when he was searching to cure 'the ailments of the heart', those terrible fits of mourning that set in.

GODFREY *begins to weep loudly.*

Father Divine, the great provider, sent his blessing via mail. And shortly thereafter Daddy was cured.

GODFREY *stops weeping and returns to reading his newspaper.*

He vowed to move nearer to Divine, to be close to God, devote his waking hours to the righteousness 'Divinely' ordained. Daddy thought Divine's Peace Mission was in Brooklyn, 'cause of a return address on a miracle elixir boasting to induce 'peace of mind'. Divine was not in Brooklyn or New York City. But that didn't diminish Daddy's love. No, he let Divine strip away his desire and demand of him a monk's devotion. This a man who never went to church and never tipped his hat to a woman, until we got to... Brooklyn.

GODFREY. What would Sweet Father say if he knew his rosebuds, on a Sunday no less, didn't have the strength or conviction to honor and respect his wishes.

ERNESTINE (*to audience*). Daddy wanted us to wear the 'V'.

ERMINA *and* ERNESTINE. Virtue, Victory and Virginity.

GODFREY. Yes indeed. Peace and blessings.

ERNESTINE (*to audience*). His words now for everything, good, bad or indifferent.

GODFREY (*by rote*). I ain't doing this 'cause I like to, I'm doing this 'cause I got to. Appreciation is like all other subtle pleasures in life, it comes with age.

A moment.

ERMINA. Well, could we at least go up to the Levys' to listen
the radio? They says so. We'd appreciate this moment all the
more.

ERNESTINE *perks up with anticipation*.

GODFREY. They's being polite… Running up there to them
white peoples every time you get a chance, they're gonna
think you don't got a proper home.

ERMINA. They old!… They don't think nothing.

GODFREY. Oh you God now, you knows what they think!

ERMINA. Nah, sir! (*Wrinkles her nose*.)

ERNESTINE (*to audience*). Mr Levy gives us a quarter on the
Sabbath to turn on the lights, the stove and of course his
smacking-new television.

ERMINA. It's practically the size of a car. For real.

GODFREY. They white people, don't know any better than to
spend their money on foolishness.

ERNESTINE (*to audience*). There you have it! 'They white' –
with those two words he can dismiss our wants, our desires,
even our simplest pleasures. 'They white.'

ERMINA *sits down and mopes, her leg shaking furiously*.

It doesn't matter that his Father Divine has gone off and
married himself a 'spotless white virgin', who remains
untarnished despite marital vows. Oh yes! There'll always be
that great divide between us and them. Divine was God, and
God was liable to do as he pleased, but you see Daddy was
just a poor colored man –

GODFREY *looks up from his newspaper*.

GODFREY *and* ERNESTINE.…from Pensacola, and I gone
out my way to keep trouble a few arms' lengths 'way. I don'
want to wind up like them Scottsboro boys, but you wouldn't
remember.

GODFREY *continues to speak;* ERNESTINE *mouths the words:*

GODFREY. Terrible mess, terrible mess.

GODFREY *takes out a little notepad and takes notes. He then returns to reading with his magnifying glass.* ERNESTINE *runs her hands across the chair as if she could feel the memory coming to life.* GODFREY *becomes choked up; he tries to restrain his sobs, but is unable to do so.*

ERNESTINE (*to audience*). Brooklyn... Evenings; listening to Daddy weep, missing Mommy and staring at the radio. A Radiola Mommy won, she guessed the number of marbles in a jar: seven hundred and two. Daddy will win playing that number some years from now. Only number he will ever play.

She and ERMINA *stare at the radio longingly. Laughter fills the stage.*

Can hear Mrs Levy upstairs in her rocking chair shifting back and forth from laughter. Can hear the television in the Friedlanders' apartment. We sit and listen to all the white laughter. Seems to us only white folks can laugh on Sunday.

Laughter fills the stage. The three stare out into space. Silence.

GODFREY. I almost forgot – (*Sing-song.*) something in my pocket for my babies.

ERMINA *and* ERNESTINE *rush over to* GODFREY*'s worn overcoat hanging over the chair.* ERNESTINE *pulls out a handful of cookies.*

ERNESTINE (*to audience*). Again, he's bought us off with cookies and shortcake. (*Savoring the words.*) Love is candied peanuts and sugar babies, day-old cinnamon buns and peach cobbler.

GODFREY. Well, maybe when I find me a 'better' job we'll, we'll, take a walk maybe, and maybe look at some television sets. I do want the best for my babies.

ERNESTINE (*to audience*). Something better is always on the horizon.

ERNESTINE *stuffs her mouth with sugar cookies, gobbling them down obsessively.*

ACT ONE

Winter

Scene One

The Crumps' living room. Lights rise on ERNESTINE. *She sits hemming a pair of her father's slacks. The radio can ever so faintly be heard through the walls.*

Lights rise on GODFREY *sitting in his armchair shining his shoes; for him, it is an act of love performed with meticulous care. In the absence of a cloth he uses a piece of newspaper to buff his shoes.*

GODFREY. Ernie, wouldn't know these was old, would ya? Would ya now? Hey, hey, the boys at the job can't help eyeing them, smart shoes like these make 'em think you more important than you is.

ERNESTINE. That so? (*To audience.*) It's Thursday. Last night a madman went on a rampage in South Brooklyn, killed a Mohawk Indian and stabbed four others with a bread knife. We're staying in.

GODFREY *shakes his head and glances at the newspaper.*

GODFREY. No reason to go out. Remember what happened to that Johnston family gal, shipped home seven of her fingers.

ERNESTINE. Nah!

GODFREY. Hear that's all that was left, no thumbs or nothing. Her mama threw herself into the baptismal waters and nearly drowned two men when they tried to rescue her. Can't even help out folks these days. (*Again, he glances down at the newspaper. He goes over to the front door and checks the lock.*) Pity! Country folk come up here and turn on each other. That's what happens when you live piled up on top of each other day in and day out. Ain't natural. (*Balls up the newspaper. In a soothing tone.*) God's done retreated from this city, I can tell you that much without being a scientist.

ERNESTINE. Where'd God go?

GODFREY (*thinks*). Philadelphia, my rosebud. (*Takes a small pad out of his pocket and jots down notes. He places the notes in a box and shoves the box beneath his chair.*)

ERNESTINE (*to audience*). We're locked inside awaiting word from Father Divine. The mailman is our deliverer.

GODFREY *stands, alert.*

GODFREY (*anxious*). The mailman here yet?

ERNESTINE. That's the third time you asked me today, sir.

GODFREY. I thought I heard you say so –

ERNESTINE. Nah, sir.

GODFREY (*excited*). Well now, I's expecting the *New Day* paper and a little word from Sweet Father. Been putting all these questions to him, it's only a matter of time before he answers. (*Earnestly.*) Peace will come.

The sound of the Levys turning the radio dial. Laughter, then gunshots, emanate from behind the wall.

We all know who done it, Mrs Levy. It's the doctor. I wish she'd turn it down, can't concentrate. It ain't good enough for white folks just to have a television, they got to let the whole neighborhood know.

ERMINA *enters casually with the mail. She thumbs through the pile.*

ERMINA. Mailman says if you leave 'im a dollar in the box he'll make sure you git your mail in the mornings like the white folk do.

GODFREY. Morning. Evening. Ain't a dollar difference to me. Whatcha got? The *New Day* come?

ERMINA *slowly picks through the mail.*

ERMINA. Look here! From home for me. (*Takes a deep whiff of the envelope, then tucks it lovingly into her skirt.*)

GODFREY. Smells good now, he won't remember your name by summer.

ERMINA *continues picking through the mail.* GODFREY *laughs to himself.*

The *New Day* come?

ERMINA. Oooo! Ernie! What I got? Look like that pattern for your graduation dress finally here. Bet you dying to see it. I bet it pretty. (*Examines the envelope. She keeps it away from* ERNESTINE.) It feel nice. Feel expensive.

ERNESTINE. Give me!

GODFREY. Expensive? What's that there?

ERMINA *tosses the pattern to* ERNESTINE.

ERMINA. You gonna tell him?... Well, if you ain't, I will. (*Defiantly.*) Mommy promised Ernie a graduation dress and she gonna need some money for the fabric. (*To* ERNESTINE.) All right, it been said!

ERNESTINE. Ermina!

GODFREY. You graduating?

ERNESTINE *nods.* GODFREY *breaks into a smile.*

Nah... A first. You really gonna graduate? You're gonna be a high-school graduate like Percy Duncan, Roberta Miles, Sarah Dickerson, Elmore Sinclair, Chappy Phillips and Ernestine Crump. Lawd, I got a high-school graduate in my living room.

ERNESTINE, *bashful, covers her face.*

ERNESTINE. Not quite yet!

GODFREY. Why didn't you say something?

ERNESTINE. Didn't I?

A moment. GODFREY, *embarrassed, takes out his notepad.*

GODFREY....The *New Day* come?

ERNESTINE *expectantly tears open the envelope.*
Delighted, she inspects the pattern. ERMINA *holds up an*
official-looking envelope.

ERMINA. The *New Day* come.

GODFREY *breaks into a broad smile.* ERMINA *passes*
GODFREY *the envelope.*

GODFREY. Glory be! Been expecting this for a week now.
Gals, gather round. (*Takes in a deep breath, then rips into the*
envelope with an unbridled pleasure. He pulls the huge
magnifying glass from his jacket pocket and begins to read
with difficulty.) Peace Angel... (*Beaming.*) He called me an
angel. (*Basks in the heavenly glow of the Peace Mission.*
Reading.) Peace Angel... You-are-one-of-the bl-bl-ess.
(*Hands the letter to* ERNESTINE.)

ERNESTINE (*reading*). Blessed. Peace Angel, you are one of
the blessed. Your positive visu... visu... visual-i-zation has
materialized into a response to your letter. Your honesty
touched me. STRENGTH! You speak of being a poor man,
being a colored man, being a man without prospects.

GODFREY *nods emphatically.*

You speak of Jim Crow. COURAGE!

GODFREY. COURAGE!

ERNESTINE (*reading*). We know that there are no differences
between the races in this Kingdom, and that segregation is
the creation of the ignorant to punish those who are in touch
with God –

GODFREY. What's that?

ERMINA *rips open her letter.*

ERNESTINE (*reading*)....segregation is the creation of the ignorant to punish those who are in touch with God. That God who is a living vital force moving through you.

GODFREY. Oh yes. Go on. Go on.

ERNESTINE (*reading*). ATONE! You, who have escaped the hold of passion and other temptations that corrupt the purity of the spirit. Remember celibacy, peace and Godliness are all that I ask of you! ABSTAIN! (*A moment.*) ALERT! I have considered your request and decided to bestow upon one of my devoted disciples beautiful names for your family. Names that God will immediately recognize and open up to a direct line of communication. All that said and done, I give you the names Godfrey Goodness –

GODFREY (*tries it on*). Godfrey Goodness!

ERNESTINE (*reading*). For your eldest, Darling Angel. And your baby, Devout Mary.

GODFREY *smiles at* ERMINA*; horrified, she mouths the name.*

JOIN US AT THE HOLY COMMUNION BANQUET! The Kingdom awaits you. REMEMBER! HEED! VIRTUE! Life is a feast, but unfortunately, food still costs money and I know you won't let us starve. Peace and Blessings, Father Divine, Philadelphia, Pennsylvania, United States of America.

GODFREY. Ain't that beautiful? THERE! He speaks the truth! From God's mouth to our ears.

ERMINA. Not me, Miss Devout Mary. (*Sucks her teeth.*) What's wrong with Ermina Crump? No way I's gonna be called Miss Devout Mary. What kinda first name is Devout? What sorta boy is gonna wanna ask out a gal named Devout Mary?

GODFREY. Well, you know where Father stands on that.

ERNESTINE (*to audience*). Is he speaking for himself or Father Divine? Ain't always clear. I like being a Crump, was just getting used to being a Crump.

GODFREY (*flabbergasted*). We're now part of his flock, we're capable of entering the Kingdom. (*In a heavenly daze, he reaches into his wallet and counts out his money.*) This is just about the best news I've heard. (*A moment. In a broad, theatrical gesture.*) My Angels, this calls for a celebration. What are you waiting for, go on and get dressed up, we're going out... to the movies!

ERNESTINE (*to audience*). At least I wish he had said that, but he sat and counted his money until it was time to go to work.

GODFREY *sits down and counts his money.*

You ever have the feeling of floating out of your body, entering the Milky Way and getting stuck in it just as it's curdling? (*Tucks the pattern under her arm.*)

Scene Two

probably modern views like the girls

Lights rise on LILY ANN 'SISTER' GREEN *standing in the Crumps' doorway; she is wearing a smartly tailored suit and sparkling white gloves. Her hat is cocked to the side and she smokes a cigarette. Her eyes are concealed behind the thick-rimmed bebop sunglasses popular at the time. She is a nonconformist, a 'dangerous woman'.* LILY *takes out a tissue, spits into it and extinguishes her cigarette.*

Lights rise on the living room. ERMINA *stands by the open door;* ERNESTINE *is sitting.*

disruption to 'status-co' by being 'different'

LILY. Didn't you hear me ringing the bell, nearly froze my ass out there. (*She displays her legs.*) These stockings, thank God for 'em, just ain't no competition for this weather. Remind me, take a note, need for weather-resistant stockings. Period. Stop! (*To* ERMINA.) Ernestine, is that my gal?

different views about the glory to godfrey / against christian views

ERNESTINE (*to audience*). And there now is Aunt Lily, the
first colored woman we'd seen dressed up like a white lady.
Smart looking and posture straight. She'd been to Harlem...
For us country folk that is the equivalent of reaching the
promised land.

LILY. Ernestine, is that my gal?

ERMINA. Ermina! (*Shuts the door.*)

LILY. But haven't you grown. Ladyish and whatnot. How's my
baby doing? Where's my hug?

ERMINA. Don't know who you is. Can't be giving out loving
to anybody that ask.

LILY *laughs*. GODFREY *enters to investigate the noise*.

LILY. Ain't that the truth. (*Strikes a pose, then takes off her coat
and throws it across the chair.*)

ERMINA. Who you?

LILY. Who I? Precious! If that ain't a question! It's me, your
Aunt Lily, Sister.

ERMINA *takes a long hard look*. GODFREY *gawks*.

(*Tentatively.*) Now Godfrey, ain't you got words for me?

GODFREY. Sister Lily? Sister Lily Ann Green?

LILY. Who else? Never thought you'd bring your country ass
on up here. You ole alligator bait. But don't you look...
good, Daddy.

LILY *walks over and embraces* GODFREY. *He stiffens
awkwardly, uncomfortable with the display of affection.*
GODFREY *takes a few steps backward and looks down at
the ground.*

GODFREY. I'll be damned! This here is your mama's sister.
Remember?

The girls do not respond.

LILY. That's all right. Memories need maintenance. I won't hold it against y'all. You're still 'y'all', 'cause some folks come North get all siddity on – (*Relishes*.) 'y'all'.

GODFREY *sits, then stands.*

GODFREY. Lawd, I've gotten so used to seeing strangers, barely know what to do with a familiar face. You're looking... smart, Sister Lily.

LILY. Now don't tell me you're surprised!

GODFREY (*jokes in a familiar way*). Used up all my surprise on the first day in Brooklyn. Ain't surprised, pleased though. Some pleasures you never stop looking forward to.

LILY (*flirtatiously*). Well now! That tongue still got a taste of honey.

An awkward moment. GODFREY *looks away from* LILY, *who smiles seductively.*

GODFREY. Ain't heard no word from you since... since... Well. (*Bows his head, unable to continue*.) We tried to track you down up there in Harlem. Ain't like a small town where your bizness is a matter of public record.

LILY (*amused*). This the big city, Godfrey, don't want everybody to know ya. They got names for women like that. Oh hell, that's why there's the telephone... But I forgot ya from the country, probably don't know how to use the telephone. (*Cackles*.) And don't think it was easy to find 'y'all'. Do like to say it, 'y'all'. I can smell the orange blossom and the pig roasting on the spit... Look at ya, I can track down a fine-looking Negro halfway across the state.

GODFREY. Now... don't... don't –

LILY. Don't get bashful on me. Gals, me and your daddy go back to –

GODFREY. It's been quite a –

LILY. Still wearing them shoes.

GODFREY *peers down at his perfectly shined shoes.*

I must admit they sure do have a fine shine.

LILY *winks at the girls. They giggle.*

GODFREY. I keep 'em up.

Laughing, LILY *takes off her gloves and tosses them on the table.*

Why don't you take a load off your feet?

LILY. Thank ya, I thought you had lost your manners. (*As she prepares to sit, she notices the picture of Sandra over the mantle. She goes over to the picture. Suddenly sober:*) Sandra. (*Takes off her hat.*) I'm sorry. I couldn't make it down for the funeral. My heart was there with 'y'all'. I cried for nearly two weeks straight. She was a special woman, I always said that. (*A moment, as she covers her eyes. She whimpers, then recovers her composure.*)

GODFREY. Great loss…

LILY *forces out a smile.* ERNESTINE *studies her aunt.*

I told you about staring, Darling.

LILY *notices and shows off her outfit.*

LILY (*breaking the silence*). Ya like my suit?

ERNESTINE *nods.*

I bought it on Fifth Avenue, sure did, to spite those white gals. You know how they hate to see a Negro woman look better than they do. It's my own little subversive mission to outdress them whenever possible. Envy is my secret weapon, babies. If ya learn anything from your auntie, let it be that.

GODFREY. So, how come you ain't stopped over sooner?

LILY. Well, ya know how it gets! (*Lights up another cigarette as she takes a perfunctory look about the apartment.*)

GODFREY. Thought you was lost up in Harlem. Selling books and whatnot.

LILY. Was. Changed my plans. Books, with the television I'm told there's no future in them. I'm… an 'etymologist' now.

GODFREY. You don't say!

ERNESTINE. Really?

LILY. Nearly broke my neck with the studies. Well, somebody had to break the barrier, let those white boys know we saying what we please.

GODFREY. How about that. Always said you was the clever one.

ERMINA. What do a et–

LILY. I ain't gonna bore you with the details. I'll leave it at that.

She grabs her stomach. GODFREY *takes out his little pad and jots down some notes.*

Oh chile, listen to it, if that ain't my stomach saying hello.

GODFREY. Oh well, we… we ain't prepared nothing for dinner yet. As a matter of fact, you… you our first visitor… (*A moment. He impulsively straightens the furniture. Stops.*) Darling Angel! We got any fixings for Sister?

ERNESTINE. I'm sure I can find something, Daddy.

LILY. Chile, don't go out your way. I ain't that hungry. (*A beat.*) Whatever ya got will be fine.

ERNESTINE *turns to leave.* LILY *reaches out to* ERNESTINE.

Ernestine, you better not leave this room without giving your aunt some sugar.

ERNESTINE *bashfully approaches* LILY *and gives her a hug.* LILY *pinches* ERNESTINE's *buttocks.*

What's that? I don't remember that being there last time. But haven't you gotten big! And look at those boobies! Bigger than mine and ya how old? Ya better watch yourself, you're liable to attract ya a grown-up man.

NO BOUNDRIES, FUNNY

LILY *shimmies, shaking her shoulders and breasts. Aghast,*
ERNESTINE *covers her breasts with her arms.* LILY
laughs. GODFREY *laughs with discomfort.*

ERNESTINE. I'm gonna go and see what's in the kitchen.

LILY. Now gal, don't want to have to take out this suit another
inch... Something light.

ERNESTINE *exits into the kitchen with her arms covering
her breasts.*

And Godfrey, you going to leave my bags out in the
hallway?

GODFREY. Bags? You going somewhere?

LILY. Not anymore.

GODFREY. Whatcha mean?

LILY. Oh hell, Godfrey, you know what I mean.

She chuckles to herself. ERMINA *gawks.*

It do seem colder in Brooklyn, but don't it though?... Didn't
see a Negro face between here and 116th. HELLO white
peoples! (*Waves. A moment.*) Living in their midst do have a
way of wearing down your stamina. (*Pats* ERMINA *on the
shoulder, then strolls around the apartment. She runs her
hand across the furniture.*) Never did have taste, Godfrey.

LILY *sinks into the chair.* ERMINA *plops down next to her.*
LILY *swings her arm around* ERMINA.

GODFREY. But I see it's good enough to sit on.

LILY. You know how it is! These tired hams. And look at you,
just standing there like you lost your tongue. What you got to
sip on? I need a drink.

GODFREY. We... we don't keep liquor in this house.

LILY *bursts into laughter.*

LILY. Oh ya a Christian now?

GODFREY. Well –

(handwritten annotation: UNHEARD OF ... IN THIS HOUSE)

LILY. Oh please, Godfrey, don't make me sick. Gimme a drink, will ya, goddamnit!

ERMINA*'s eyes grow big.* LILY *continues to laugh.*
GODFREY *is horrified.*

You really a Christian? (*She peers at the portrait of Father Divine.*) Oh I see, the Peace Mission, Father Divine. He still alive and playing God? *(handwritten annotation: CYNICAL ABOUT FATHER DIVINE)*

GODFREY. Sweet Father Divine, he found me down in Florida and his word carried us up here. I'd still be mourning over my biscuits in the Nortons' kitchen if –

LILY *straightens her clothing.*

LILY. I'm touched, Mr Crump –

ERMINA. Goodness.

LILY. Goodness. I recall a certain Saturday at the juke –

GODFREY. Please.

LILY. Please, nonsense. You do remember the juke joint. Don't tell me you've given up everything? Everything? Hell, I'm surprised.

A moment.

GODFREY. Now we both been surprised. And you? You still up there fooling with –

LILY. Go on say it, tongue won't fall out. The communist party, amongst other things.

ERMINA *giggles.*

Oh, you find that funny? (*Earnestly.*) I ain't laughing. I suppose ya happy with what you got, a bit of nothing. Sure, I was happy at your age, 'a little pickaninny' selling hotcakes to the fishermen. Taking pennies from poor people ain't a job, it's a chore. This may be New York, but this still the basement. Don't none of those crackers want to share any bit

(handwritten annotation: SHE'S A communist)

of power with us. That's what it's about. Red Scare, should be called Black Scare.

GODFREY. I wish you wouldn't conniggerate in front of the gal.

LILY. You act like I'm saying dirty words. Worker! Revolution! Proletariat! There! Christian!

GODFREY. This communism thing a bit frightening to this young one.

LILY. Ain't no more frightening than Jim Crow. I said my 'peace'.

GODFREY. Go on! 'Cause talk like that keeps company with the door closing behind you. You know something about that.

LILY. Watch yourself! I promised Nana I'd look after these gals for her. She don't think it's proper that a man be living alone with his daughters once they sprung bosom. I'm here out of sense of duty. So relax, you've always been tight in the chest. Breathe, breathe. There you go. God won't strike you down for relaxing. (*A moment. Smiling.*) Well, could I get a soda pop at least, spent half the day underground.

ERMINA (*cheerfully*). I'll get it. (*She exits.*)

LILY (*yelling after*). Thank you, sweet thing.

She and GODFREY *have a tense, awkward moment, not quite sure what to say to each other.*

Nice-looking gal. Precious.

LILY *smiles seductively;* GODFREY *looks away, then takes out his little pad and jots down some notes.*

LILY. What do you keep writing down?

GODFREY. Oh, nothing, just questions. Things I want to ask Father Divine when he comes to New York for the Holy Communion.

OPPRESSIVE

LILY. Oh! And I thought it was something interesting.

Unnoticed, ERNESTINE *reenters the room with a sandwich.*

GODFREY. You ain't changed a bit.

LILY. Thank ya.

GODFREY. That ain't how I meant it.

LILY *flicks her ashes on top of an old magazine.* GODFREY *retrieves an ashtray for her.*

LILY (*noticing* ERNESTINE). Oh, there ya go.

ERNESTINE *places the sandwich on the table.* LILY *greedily examines the sandwich, not entirely pleased with the offerings, but nevertheless hungry.*

Let me see what you got me to eat. Didn't have no mayonnaise?

ERMINA *returns with a glass of soda.* LILY *drinks it down, then ravenously bites into the sandwich, fighting to force down the half-chewed chunks of food.*

MMMMmmm. That hit the spot. (*Embarrassed, she looks* ERMINA *over. To* ERMINA.) Thank you, sweet-smelling thing, that's nice at your age. You must be fifteen.

KNOWING SOMETHING IN HER BONES,

ERMINA *nods.*   *INFORMAL*

KNOWING THEY'LL

THAT RESULT

How'd I know? Prescience is what carried me up here. Prescience, my dear chile. It runs deep through our African veins; take a note, tell family story one day, period, stop! Ain't ya pretty. She looks just like Sandra. Don't she?

ERMINA. You think so?

ERNESTINE. Back home everybody say I look like my mother also.

LILY. That so?… Are my bags okay in the hallway?

She bites into the sandwich. GODFREY *reluctantly exits to retrieve* LILY*'s bags from the hallway.* ERNESTINE *studies her aunt with a childlike infatuation.*

VERY DIRECT

ERNESTINE. You really my mommy's sister?

LILY nods.

I don't see it.

LILY. It ain't the first time I heard that. But I am your mama's sister, don't let the style fool ya, take away this suit and there's still a little country.

GODFREY reenters with three enormous suitcases. He drops the suitcases at LILY's feet.

GODFREY. What you got in here anyway?

LILY. My life, darling, and when ya look at it in those terms them bags ain't that heavy. Are they now? (*She cracks up.*)

GODFREY (*mumbled*). I suppose ya gonna stay. (*He carries LILY's bags into the bedroom.*)

LILY. Only if you insist.

Lights fade on everyone but ERNESTINE.

ERNESTINE (*to audience*). Down home when Rosalind's mother came back from New York smoking cigarettes and her face painted up, the minister declared it the end of the world, oh, I remember the horror he instilled. He preached his longest sermon on the nature of sin. But I'd confronted sin tonight and it didn't seem half bad.

THE GIRLS LIKE LILY,

LIKE THE RELATED MENTALITY

Scene Three

The Crumps' kitchen. ERMINA sits in a straight-back chair. LILY heats a hot iron comb on the stove; she takes it off, then wipes the hot comb in a towel and applies it to ERMINA's head. ERNESTINE reads a magazine.

MATERNAL INSTINCT ROLE

ERNESTINE (*to audience*). You place two single beds together it becomes big enough for three. The mathematics of the

Crump household. I don't know how I got pushed to the middle, stuck on the crack. Just like down home, where the Hendersons were known to squeeze seven to a bed. Many a night we did ponder that puzzle.

ERMINA. Why'd you lose your job?

LILY. Well, babies, a Negro woman with my gumption don't keep work so easily. It's one of the hazards of being an independent thinker. If I've ever had me a job for more than a few weeks then I knew it was beneath me. You see what I'm saying?

[handwritten: TROUBLE MAKER MAYBE]

ERMINA. Ernie wanna be a movie star.

ERNESTINE. Hush up!

LILY. 'Darling Angel, the star of stage and screen, the virginal vixen.' (*Laughs*.)

ERNESTINE. But I'd change my name to something special. Like 'Sylvie Montgomery'. Or 'Laura Saint Germaine'; that's French.

LILY. Well, pardon me, Miss Bette Davis, when'd you git to be so big and black?

ERMINA. Ooooooo.

ERNESTINE *wraps a towel around her hair, feigning brushing long silky hair.*

ERNESTINE (*playfully*). It runs in the family. But don't you worry yourself. When I'm onscreen I sure can act very white. That's why I'm a star.

LILY. If only they knew you began as a poor colored child.

ERNESTINE. Imagine that.

LILY *laughs*.

LILY. Imagine that. Miss Bette, I must say, I like ya a wee bit better, just a wee bit now, as a colored child. When's your next picture? I hear it's a romance.

A moment. *[handwritten: SUGGESTS THE IDEA OR EQUAL, HAPPY TO FANTISISE]*

ERMINA. She ain't never gonna make no romance until she get rid of some of the butt.

ERNESTINE *sucks her teeth*.

LILY. Hush! Romance is overrated. I've known too many women who relinquished their common sense for a dose of… romance.

ERMINA. Sister, why ain't you been married?

LILY *laughs long and hard*.

LILY. You're just filled with questions. 'Cause I ain't. (*Tugs* ERMINA*'s head straight, wielding the hot comb like a weapon*.)

ERMINA. Nobody ask you?

LILY. Nobody ask me… Besides, I never plan to marry. How you like that? I'm exerting my own will, and since the only thing ever willed for me was marriage, I choose not to do it. And why take just one man, when you can have a lifetime full of so many. Listen up, that may be the best advice I give you babies. And you needn't share that little pearl of wisdom with your daddy. Now, Ermina, sit still!

ERNESTINE (*to audience*). We were Lily's family now, kinda like buying flowers from a store without having to plant the seeds.

ERMINA *squirms in the chair*.

LILY. Sit still, don't fight me on this. Choose your battles carefully, chile, a nappy head in this world might as well fly the white flag and surrender!

ERNESTINE (*to audience*). She'd talk constantly about 'a revolution' from the kitchen. I's always wondered when this revolution was going to begin and would I have to leave school to fight along her side.

LILY. We're at war, babies. You don't want to be walking around school with a scar across your forehead. You want people to think your hair's naturally straight. That it flows in the wind.

ERNESTINE. How are they gonna think that?

LILY. Pass me the Dixie Peach. When I'm finished you're gonna look just like a little Indian girl.

> ERNESTINE *reaches under the chair and passes* LILY *the jar of Dixie Peach hair pomade.* LILY *rolls up her sleeves.*

ERNESTINE (*to audience*). Would this revolution pit Negro against white, rich against poor? And just how many would die?

LILY. If Jennifer Johnson –

ERNESTINE. Jones.

LILY. Well, that white lady star walked through that door right now, she wouldn't look no better than you or I. She'd look just like them cracker women with their bad teeth and gutter ways. Frankly, I git tired of them telling you how you supposed to look good. I can turn a man's head in any part of this country, hairpiece or not. Ermina, sit still and maybe I can take a little bit of the nap out this kitchen.

> LILY *presses the hot comb against the back of* ERMINA*'s hair.* ERMINA *lets out a terrible wail.*

ERNESTINE. Just like Mommy used to do.

LILY. She never could handle a hot comb, bless her heart.

> LILY *presses the comb to* ERMINA*'s head;* ERMINA *wails.*

ERMINA. You trying to kill me?

LILY. Vanity is a weapon. I'm not trying to kill ya, I'm trying to make ya beautiful enough to kill others. There's the difference. (*Lights a cigarette.*)

ERMINA. My hair's gonna smell like smoke.

LILY. Hush up, it's good for it, adds texture. Sweetness, open the door so your daddy won't smell the smoke. He can sniff it out hours later like a goddamn hound dog.

Lights fade on all but ERNESTINE.

ERNESTINE (*to audience*). Smothered in gossamer smoke and dizzying assertions, I wondered, had her revolution already begun? So I went down to the public library round my way, 'Revolution, American; Revolutionary War; Revolution, French'. But no Negro Revolution. I did find twenty entries on communism in the card catalog, but no books on the shelves. The teacher said, 'Select a topic that's close to you.' My essay was entitled 'The Colored Worker in the United States'; the mistake was using the word 'worker' too liberally. The principal called in Daddy Goodness and told him to stop mingling with the Jews at his job and everything would be all right. Daddy didn't bother to tell him that his coworkers were all colored. And the Jews on our block won't speak to us. Well, except the Levys, who if they didn't talk to us they'd have to sit in the darkness on Friday night.

Lights rise on GODFREY *shining his shoes in the living room.* LILY *sits in the armchair reading a movie magazine.*

GODFREY (*hushed*). Whole school thinks I'm a communist. It's all your fault, ya know.

LILY. And I suppose I'm to blame for segregation, war and polio as well.

GODFREY. You can't ever leave well enough alone. It's fine for you and your smart set, but I'm a working man gotta ride the bus each morning.

LILY. Surprised you ain't walking as tight as you are.

GODFREY. Don't change the subject on me.

LILY. Well, hell, Godfrey, I ain't said nothing about nothing. I can't help it if that child got eyes and ears, and a mind that ain't limited to a few pages in the Bible. I ain't seen you this spirited since I got here... in fact, I think being a communist agrees with you.

LILY *gives* GODFREY *a few playful jabs.* GODFREY *feigns laughter.*

GODFREY. That's funny! Try telling that to the fellas at work, ain't none of them speaking to me. (*Pointing to* LILY.) This is your doing. Got that old bad magic rubbing off on us.

LILY. Don't get superstitious on me. (*Laughs.*)

GODFREY. My little voice told me something like this could happen.

LILY. That little voice got you wound too tight! Shucks, I think you need to come uptown with me and get a little taste of reality.

GODFREY. Sister, I don't care what you think, that's the honest-to-God truth. But I do care what my gals think. (*To* ERNESTINE.) Darling, you gonna have to go up to school and apologize.

ERNESTINE. Why's that, Daddy?

LILY. Ya gonna make the chile do that? Punish her for having thoughts. How are we ever gonna get ahead? Have you read it? It might be a fine piece of writing, Godfrey. Look here, it says –

GODFREY. I don't care what it say, but it upset that white teacher and she seemed like a smart lady.

LILY *makes a show of sitting down to read the essay.*

LILY. I like the way it starts already. Simple, don't bother with them highfalutin words.

GODFREY *snatches the essay out of* LILY's *hand.*

GODFREY. She gonna apologize!

ERNESTINE *shakes her head furiously.*

And I'm going to tell you once, then I'm gonna leave it alone: we were doing just fine without your sorta learning. We don't want and we don't need it.

LILY. Well, I promised my mama I'd look after these babies. They need a woman's voice in this house, that's what they need.

GODFREY. Maybe you ain't the right woman.

LILY *stares long and hard, fighting back the urge to respond.* GODFREY *turns away from her and jots down some notes in his pad.*

LILY. That's right! Go on, ask Father Divine! Ask him what to think.

Lights begin to fade on a simmering GODFREY, *leaving* ERNESTINE *and a laughing* LILY *in separate pools of light.*

ERNESTINE. I... Darling Angel, apologize for anything in my essay that might suggest that communism is a good thing. My intent was to deal with the labor movement in the United States, which primarily consists of God-fearing patriotic Americans dedicated to improving the conditions for the working man.

[*handwritten annotation: ∩ IRONRY*]

She crosses her heart. The National Anthem plays.

I pledge allegiance to the flag of the United States of America... (*Her eyes cloud over with tears.*)

LILY. I never stand for the National Anthem, don't even know the words. But ya know the tune that git me to my feet every time, that Charlie Parker playing 'Salt peanuts, salt peanuts'. Chile, I practically conceded to God when he took his sax on up that scale.

A bebop version of 'Salt Peanuts' plays. LILY *exits. Lights continue to fade on* GODFREY.

ERNESTINE (*to audience*). Daddy had become a communist by inference. His fear of God replaced by the fear of the government. If he'd read the essay, then he might have fought a little harder when he was passed over for the promotion and we'd be watching television in the evenings. Down home he fought only once, when he got drunk on a barrel of sour whiskey and went on a drunken tirade. Beaten nearly senseless, he accused the white man who sold him the liquor of allowing the devil to slip into his soul. Mommy calmed his brow with witch hazel and talked him into a gentle sleep. His anger a faint memory at rest.

Scene Four

The living room. ERMINA *is dressed for a visit to the Peace Mission in a pristine white pinafore. A very drunk and disheveled* LILY *enters. She accidentally knocks into* ERNESTINE*'s dressmaker's dummy, which displays the beginnings of a white graduation dress.* LILY *catches it just as it's toppling over and does a halfhearted cha-cha with the dummy as her partner.*

LILY (*seeing* ERMINA). Oh! YOU STILL UP!

ERMINA. Shh!

LILY. WHY YA UP SO LATE?

ERMINA. It's morning.

LILY. That's what I told 'em. (*A moment.*) Where ya going? You playing doctor or something?

ERMINA. We're going to the Peace Mission. Help get ready for Sweet Father's visit.

LILY. He's finally letting you out of the house, and you're going out dressed like that. Little pixies. Oh no, not me. (*Plops down.*)

ERMINA. I don't wanna go, but Ernie won't say nothing to Daddy.

LILY. THEN WHY GO?

ERNESTINE *rushes in. She is also dressed in a pristine white pinafore.*

ERMINA. Shh! Daddy here.

LILY *cackles.*

ERNESTINE. You wanna lie down? Please, Sister, wish ya would… Don't let Daddy find you this way.

LILY. He's the one that talk to me first. He was leaning against the window smiling at me. He says he's from Cuba, but he sure didn't look like no Desi Arnaz. Black like coal… But he do speak Spanish, of course he could have learned it from a correspondence book. Right? Like my friend Janice did. He could of been right from Florida, I'm telling you. He was splendid to look at, hair like a wave breaking, good hair. It just fall flat by itself. And he wasn't no good-time boy, a real gentleman like from your movies, Ernie.

A slow mambo begins to play.

He tipped his hat and everything, asked if he could escort me home. I told him up front, 'I ain't like those gals standing big-bellied in a state line 'cause they gave themselves for an evening at the Savoy and a pair of silk stockings. I'm a grown woman with a different set of requirements. You see, Mr Cuba, I'm a thinking woman, I'm communist!' He laughed and said, 'Baby, so am I, tonight.'

She stands up. The girls look on with disbelief.

I danced the mambo. Our hips pressed together. Me and Papo.

ERNESTINE. You did what?

LILY. I danced the mambo. (*Demonstrates the steps.*) Oh, gimme your hand – (*Teasing.*) Darling Angel.

ERNESTINE. Please don't call me that.

LILY. Hell, ya dressed for the part.

The mambo music grows louder. LILY *grabs* ERNESTINE, *wrapping her wiry arm around her niece's thick frame.*

Ya stiffer than a board. Ain't you never danced up close with somebody?

ERNESTINE. Why would I want to do that?

LILY *draws* ERNESTINE *in close.*

ERMINA. Daddy ain't gonna like the mambo!

LILY. He a man, I imagine a man invented the mambo.

ERMINA. What about me? I want to do the mambo.

LILY. You too young yet, ain't supposed to get that close to a man's privates, might be a little surprise ya ain't ready for.

ERMINA *sucks her teeth.*

ERMINA. Been closer up to a boy than Ernie ever been.

ERNESTINE. You better not have.

LILY *swings* ERNESTINE *around. They continue their dance.*

LILY. Papo was all shiny and black like a new pair of patent-leather shoes. He kept whispering in my ear, '*Que Linda! Que Linda!*' How beautiful I was.

She and ERNESTINE *dance the mambo, their cheeks pressed together.*

How beautiful I was.

Blue projector light comes on and begins to flicker.

ERNESTINE (*to audience*). I want to cry. I want to be dancing with Papo. He's slender and dark like the man at the watch counter at Loesser's.

LILY *and* ERNESTINE *continue to dance an elaborate mambo. The music stops abruptly.* GODFREY *stands in the doorway, horrified.*

GODFREY. Darling, Devout, go on outside!

ERNESTINE (*to audience*). If this had been a movie, Papo would have come to Sister's rescue. In the movies, he'd have been a dashing young doctor, rather than a fishmonger. He'd have asked my daddy for Sister's hand in marriage.

ERMINA *and* ERNESTINE *scramble for their coats.*

LILY. Oh nigger, don't start with me.

GODFREY. I said, go!

ERNESTINE *and* ERMINA *stand by the door, poised to leave.*

LILY. But we're doing the mambo.

She reaches for ERNESTINE's *hand.* ERNESTINE *is tempted to take it, but* GODFREY *gives her a look of condemnation.*

I danced with the man, Godfrey. Anything else done was imagined.

GODFREY *takes* LILY's *arm to lead her to the couch.*

Are ya asking me to dance?

LILY *dances a circle around a steadfast* GODFREY.

GODFREY. Where ya stockings?

LILY *isn't wearing stockings and laughs at the discovery.*

LILY. I don't know.

GODFREY (*holding his notepad*). You been drinking?

LILY. I'm drunk.

GODFREY. You know I don't permit drinking here.

LILY. I didn't drink here. I drank before I got here. So it don't count. And Mr Goodness, don't you go off pretending like you ain't had a drink. (*To the girls.*) I remember a particular batch of moonshine that blinded him. (*Back to* GODFREY.) Groping in the darkness, I do remember ya gitting friendly with this-here thigh. (*Winks.*)

GODFREY. Hush up now, don't want the neighbors to hear. DARLING, DEVOUT, I said, go outside.

ERNESTINE. She's sorry, Daddy. She's just tired.

GODFREY. Tired my behind.

LILY *laughs again.*

Don't make this a joke. You'll git us all in trouble like –

LILY. That's what you'd have them believe. Tell them the truth... That's what this is about, ain't it? How come in your version I always start the trouble, as though I alone single-handedly brought down the ancient walls of decorum and civility in Pensacola. Oh, for God's sake, I ain't the devil, I ain't paying ya sub-minimum wage, Mr Goodness.

GODFREY. You ain't paying nothing period. And you know this wouldn't happen if you came on down to the Peace Mission; why, you'd understand that liquor and loose moral character are the cripplers of our race.

LILY. When did you get so self-righteous, Mr Goodness? You used to be able to get a good laugh out of me. Now you're all peace and blessings. (*Directed toward the girls.*) Passing judgment on me, like he's above it all. (*A moment.*) You wanna know something, I got a secret for ya. (*Whispered.*) I hate your Sweet Father.

ERNESTINE (*to audience*). Oh, she did say 'hate'. I wish she hadn't, I wish she'd said, 'I'm bothered by Father Divine' or 'I'm sickened by Father Divine'.

GODFREY (*hushed*). Pray for forgiveness, for peace of mind. You're lucky Sweet Father loves all, including those who have forsaken 'im. I wish you would go on inside and sleep off this bewitching.

LILY. Sleep it off. Damn it. I can't sleep off this bewitching any more than you can make Sandra rise from the dead or I can return home a virginal bride primed for marriage to an ignorant sharecropper. Picking fruit, damn, my fingers are hurting just thinking about it.

GODFREY. How can you be so disrespectful to Sandra's memory? (*Puts on his hat.*)

LILY. I know a few folks that would testify to the fact that you drove poor Sandra into the grave. I can't say I blame her.

GODFREY. ERNESTINE, ERMINA! You heard what I said. GO!

He grabs his daughters' arms and shoves them into the bedroom.

NOT IN FRONT OF THEM, YOU DON'T! (*Angrily approaches* LILY, *thinks, then recomposes himself.*) Were you at Sandra's side when she closed her eyes? Where were you when we put her in the ground?

LILY. I own part of that pain.

GODFREY. No, you were up North with your books and your friends and your party.

LILY. Sounds like you're jealous.

GODFREY. Not me!

LILY. Yes, I was up North with my books and friends. Why should I stay someplace that treated me like filth.

GODFREY. Treated you? And I was having a grand ole time baking cakes for Mr and Mrs Norton. (*Shaken.*) And now you're gonna stand in my home and disrespect the choices I've made.

LILY. I ain't disrespecting ya, Godfrey. Honestly. Just having fun. What have I done, seriously? 'Cause you've purged your life of passion don't mean I got to. If I go to hell, I go of my own volition, not 'cause some preacherman's words sent me there. What have all your prayers brought you anyway? A sorry pair of shoes and an apartment barely fit for human beings.

GODFREY. It ain't enough that you got the whole neighborhood thinking I'm a... (*Whispered.*) communist. Now you have to unsettle my home with your, your, your –

LILY. What would you like me to do? You want me to apologize?

She moves toward GODFREY. *She leans into him and plants a kiss. He momentarily gives in to the kiss.*

There. (*Breaks into a smile.*)

GODFREY. My gals are going to have the best. They're gonna rise above you and I. When you're on my time clock, eating out of my icebox, sleeping under my roof, Father Divine is your leader. His word is grace. You don't like it you can git the… you can leave us at peace. I left Florida for a reason, couldn't breathe, couldn't think, couldn't do nothing but go to work, make my dime and drink it down on Friday night. Then I found something that gave me inspiration, gave me strength to make a change. May not be like your change, revolution! Oh, but it do feel that big to me. It soothed my pain and that's all I want right now. It took all the strength I had to take these gals on a train, out their wooden doors and place 'em here in brick and concrete. And I think I deserve some respect and you're trying me, you're trying me.

He sniffs the air. LILY *smiles seductively.*

I smell the liquor and the sweat. I see the jukebox swirling and the cats laughing. (*Begins to laugh, lost in the memory.*) I can hear the big sister on stage hollering out her song. Go on, sing! (*Stomps his feet.*) But I ain't going there. Taste my lips puffing on a Cuba, talking out my ass.

He pulls LILY *close to him and does a few quick dance steps, then releases her.*

Feel my hands 'round a woman's hips, swaying to the beat. But I ain't there!

GODFREY *storms out the door. Lights slowly fade on a dejected* LILY *as they rise on* ERNESTINE, *swathed in the blue glow of the cinema.*

ERNESTINE (*to audience*). In the movies the clothing is always perfectly ironed, the seams even and pointed. In the movies, when families argue it is underscored by beautiful music and reconciliation. In the movies, men are heroes, broad-shouldered and impervious to danger. Their lives are perfect formulas resolved in ninety minutes. But as Daddy would say, 'They white.'

Scene Five

The blue, flickering light rises on ERNESTINE *holding a pair of galoshes in her hand. She is on the stoop in front of the Crumps' apartment.*

ERNESTINE (*to audience*). So Daddy disappeared, went off with just a jacket and a hat. He didn't even take his rubbers and it's gonna rain. It's gonna rain furiously for the next few days. That's all that will be talked about on the radio.

The blue, flickering light shifts into subway lights, which reveal GODFREY *on the IRT train. He sits with his hat pulled over his eyes, asleep.* GERTE, *a thirty-year-old German woman, sits next to him with her luggage surrounding her feet. She nudges* GODFREY. GERTE *has the posture of a film star from the thirties and the waning beauty of a showgirl.*

GERTE. Is this the Bronx?

GODFREY. This may well be the Bronx.

GERTE (*German expletive*). The gentlemen said, 'Lady, if you reach the Bronx, you know you've gone too far.'

GODFREY *pulls his hat over his eyes.* GERTE *laughs at her mistake.*

Do you know Pierre Boussard?

GODFREY. Should I?

GERTE. I have his address in New Orleans. I was told I must go to Pennsylvania Station to catch the train. (*Unfolds the address and shows it to* GODFREY.)

GODFREY. Probably the case. I wouldn't know.

GERTE. It is far, New Orleans?

GODFREY. It far.

GERTE. I'm from Germany, I recently arr–

GODFREY. How about that, you the first German I seen that ain't in a newsreel.

GERTE *shuffles in her seat.* GODFREY *moves away slightly.*

GERTE. Do you mind if I talk with you?

GODFREY. We talking already.

GERTE (*laughing*). I guess we are.

GODFREY. What, ya trying to git me in trouble?

GERTE. Have I done something wrong?

GODFREY. Oh no! Shove on, sister, I ain't one of those uptown cats. I ain't like those adventurous colored fellas. I'm a family man.

GODFREY *stands up.* GERTE *self-consciously checks to make sure all of her clothing is in order. The train pulls into the station.* GODFREY *moves away.*

GERTE. Are you getting off?

GODFREY *does not respond.*

(*Panicked.*) Should I get off here? Which way should I be going?

GODFREY. I don't know where it is ya going, ma'am.

GERTE *stands. The train pulls out.* GERTE *returns to her seat and begins to weep.* GODFREY *turns away, and eases his hat back over his eyes. A moment.*

(*Lifting his hat.*) Are you all right?

GERTE. No.

A moment.

GODFREY. Ya want a cookie?

GERTE. Thank you.

GODFREY *hands her a cookie. She greedily stuffs it in her mouth.*

May I have another?

GODFREY *gives her another cookie.*

These are good… Your wife make?

GODFREY. I made.

GERTE *manages a smile.*

Ain't so bad, you'll find your way.

GERTE *nods;* GODFREY *moves away again. The train pulls into the station.*

GERTE. You're not getting off, are you?

GODFREY. Not yet.

GERTE. Good.

GODFREY *looks down at the bags. He sits back down next to* GERTE.

GODFREY. Looks like you got the world there.

Darkness. The roar of the train. GERTE *screams. Lights rise on* GERTE *clinging to* GODFREY*'s arm.* GODFREY *looks at* GERTE *and untangles her from his arm.*

It's all right, gave me a little scare also. Look at that. Lights back on.

GERTE. I am sorry. I thought. You don't want to know what I thought.

GODFREY. It's all right, ma'am.

GERTE. Sorry… I'll stop talking to you.

A moment.

Please, may I have another cookie?

GODFREY. You hungry?

GERTE *nods.*

Well, over at the… Peace Mission. I think I'm heading that way. They'll feed you if you're hungry.

GERTE. May I follow you? I am sorry. I shouldn't have asked.

GODFREY *looks from side to side.*

GODFREY. If you like, but it's not like we'd be going there together.

GERTE *tries to straighten her clothing. She takes a quick sniff of her underarms, then returns to sitting quietly.*

GERTE (*suddenly*). I am Gerte Schulte.

GODFREY. I am Godfrey Goodness.

They shake hands timidly. GERTE *slowly retracts her hand. They quickly look away from each other.*

GERTE. I am so glad you spoke to me.

GODFREY. Well, it looks like we were looking for the same place after all.

GERTE *and* GODFREY *are basked in a heavenly glow; then, the lights fade on them. Lights rise on* ERNESTINE *and* LILY *on the stoop.* LILY *wears a rain slicker and carries a bucket.*

ERNESTINE (*to audience*). The water backed up in the yard. What a sight, Lily in her high heels trying to clear the drain, too proud to ask any of the neighbors for help.

LILY. Ya ask white folks for help, and they turn it 'round on ya in a second. Self-deter-ma-nision, there's an uptown word for ya to digest.

ERNESTINE (*to audience*). Even the drainpipe had become part of the struggle. Then the oak tree at the corner blew down the telephone line and all the neighbors gathered to watch the workmen carve up the three-hundred-year-old tree. 'If that ain't a sign,' said Lily. It took them three days to clear it and still no sign of Daddy. Our tears salted over and caked our brown faces gray. Lily chipped away the bits of crust with a butter knife, soothing us with the hope that with the death of a great oak comes life.

Scene Six

The empty living room. The front door opens slowly. A cautious, nervous GODFREY *steps in carrying a suitcase. He stands for a moment before speaking.*

GODFREY (*sing-song*). GOT SOMETHING IN MY POCKET FOR MY BABIES!

A moment. GODFREY *tips his hat to Father Divine.* ERMINA *and* ERNESTINE *enter. They stare at their father, not quick to forgive.*

Ain't ya happy to see me?

ERMINA*'s leg begins to twitch.*

ERNESTINE. Where you been?

GODFREY. Can I get me a hug or some sugar at least? (*Spreads his arms imploringly.*)

ERNESTINE. I don't know.

GODFREY. What about ya, Devout?

ERMINA*'s leg stops twitching. She quickly approaches her father and throws her arms around his waist.*

ERNESTINE. Ermina!

ERMINA *reaches into her father's pocket and retrieves a cookie.*

ERMINA. WELL!

GODFREY. That's my girl... Had to clear my head, bring some order to things. I think everything's gonna be all right... I got someone for y'all to meet.

GERTE, *wearing a haggard smile, steps into the apartment carrying a suitcase. She clears her throat.*

Darling, Devout, this is Gerte.

ERNESTINE *and* ERMINA *stare at* GERTE.

My new wife.

The girls are dumbfounded, caught off-guard by the declaration. GERTE *gracefully extends her hand as if practiced.*

GERTE (*by rote*). I'm very pleased to meet you. I'm sure we will get on fondly. I've heard charming stories about you both. Devout, you are as pretty as your father said, and Darling, congratulations are in order for completing your studies this coming summer.

Both girls gasp. GERTE *turns to* GODFREY *to ensure that she has produced the correct information; he nods affectionately.*

ERMINA. She white!

Awkward silence.

GODFREY. Well, should we all sit?

ERMINA. Why? She won't be white if we sit down?

GODFREY *clumsily fumbles for* GERTE's *hand. The gesture is mechanical, the mark of unfamiliarity.*

GERTE. It is a lovely apartment.

GODFREY. She won't bite. Will ya?

GERTE *lets out a deep belly laugh. The girls continue to stare contemptuously at* GERTE, *who slaps* GODFREY's *hand.*

GERTE. I told you not to make me laugh.

GERTE *continues to laugh heartily, without taking a breath for air.* ERNESTINE *and* ERMINA *stare at her.*

ERNESTINE (*to audience*). Oh God, did she have to be German? If he had to have a white lady, why not a French lady or an English lady like the demure Olivia de Havilland with her modest downward glance. But there she is like Marlene Dietrich, a cold bitter whore laughing in our doorway. She might as well be wearing a satin tuxedo and blowing smoke in our faces.

GODFREY. Ain't you going to say anything?

ERMINA. Ya drunk? Ya all right?

GODFREY. Don't stand there looking foolish, say something.

ERMINA. Huh?

GODFREY. Darling.

GERTE *extends her hand a second time*.

Take her hand.

ERNESTINE *reluctantly seizes* GERTE*'s hand, giving it a hard shake*.

ERNESTINE. Mommy wouldn't like this one bit. Oh no! Mommy ain't even dead a year.

GERTE *ceases to be amused*.

GERTE. I'm sorry. I lost my mother when I was young.

LILY *stands in the doorway*.

ERNESTINE. I don't want you here!

GODFREY. Don't say that, Darling.

ERMINA*'s leg begins to jerk uncontrollably*.

LILY. What's this all about, Godfrey?

GODFREY (*defensive*). We met, we fell in love, we married.

Blackout.

ACT TWO

Spring

Scene One

Limbo. ERNESTINE, *dressed in her finest clothing, stands in a circle of light. She wears a huge black 'V' sewn above her bosom.* LILY, *in the living room, gathers some of her personal objects, including her suit.*

ERNESTINE (*to audience*). The revolution still hadn't come even though I peered out the window each day in anticipation. Gerte swept the stoop every day at four, Mrs Levy turned on the television at five, Daddy went to work at six and Aunt Lily prepared to go uptown to commune with 'possibility and the future' at seven.

LILY. How I look?

LILY, *dressed up, peers in a compact mirror and applies lipstick.*

ERNESTINE (*to audience*). Not a word, not a whisper of Daddy's 'Divine' inspiration. Sister was the portrait of calm.

LILY *fixes her hat.*

LILY (*suddenly nostalgic*). The scent of the ocean used to travel up to our porch on the back of a nice summer breeze, your mama and I would stand patiently for hours, courting. The boys had to take a number just to knock on the front door, and they'd bring us withered hibiscus. Everyone always said I would be the one to marry early, 'cause I was considered the better looking of the two. Ain't it funny how things work out. Well, hell, I didn't like standing still, and you gotta stand still long enough to attract yourself a man, I suppose. (*Laughs.*) Never been interested, outgrew the notion of a

family back in '47. How I look? Like an agitator? You ain't
listening to me nohow. I'm talking to myself. (*Takes out a
flask and takes a quick drink.*) You go on to your Peace
Mission, I'm not sure Father Divine will understand the
mystique of this pretty face. I don't think he'll appreciate
that I'd rather spend his dollar on a bottle of bourbon. It's a
small price to pay for salvation. (*A moment.*) She going?

ERNESTINE (*to audience*). Whenever a good dose of reality is
about to set in, Father Divine descends. Why have conflict
when you can feast?

*Lights rise on the Peace Mission. An immense, elaborately
set banquet table adorns the stage. The Crump family,
including GERTE, are dressed in their finest clothing. Like
ERNESTINE, ERMINA also wears a huge 'V'. The family
is dwarfed by the table crowded with prodigious portions of
food concealed in silver dishes. GODFREY reads over his
list of questions for Father Divine.*

GODFREY. I don't know what question to ask Sweet Father
first. I've planned this so long, I'm shaking.

ERNESTINE (*to audience*). So it is. Awaiting Sweet Father's
arrival. Searching for salvation in the tender juices of a
mutton chop layered in our favorite mint jelly, God speaks
the language of our stomachs.

GODFREY. Amen!

ERNESTINE. Any doubt of Sweet Father's power is allayed by
the rapture incited by the lemon tarts at the end of the table.

*ERNESTINE greedily eyes the platter at the end of the table.
The Crump family sits, patiently preparing to feast. GERTE
peeks into the containers.*

GERTE. Relish, brisket –

GODFREY. Haven't seen a meal like this since my uncle Milan
passed away and don't you know none of his lady friends
would be outdone at the wake. But didn't we find a touch of
bliss in his wife's sorrow. (*Beaming.*) Isn't this wonderful?

ERNESTINE (*to audience*). The porcelain dish of butter is now the sacred vessel of salvation.

GERTE. Is so much food necessary? There are starving children in Europe. (*Lifts the lids of containers.*) Pudding, dumplings –

ERNESTINE (*to audience*). We're eating for all mankind.

GODFREY. A communion.

GERTE (*overwhelmed by the abundance*). Gravy, peas –

ERNESTINE (*to audience*). Then, suddenly, in the middle of the feast –

GERTE *rises from behind the table and sheds her dress to reveal a slinky white cocktail dress. She climbs onto the table as music swells. A bright spotlight hits* GERTE *as she slowly traipses across the table singing 'Falling in Love Again'.* GODFREY, *aghast, ceases to eat.* GERTE *completes the song. All fall silent.*

Well, at least I wish she had, but there she sat, eagerly awaiting Sweet Father's arrival and making Daddy proud.

GERTE *returns to her seat.*

We probably would've eaten ourselves into oblivion, but Sweet Father's Duesenberg took a flat outside of Trenton.

ERMINA (*whispered*). If he God, why don't he sprout wings and fly here.

ERNESTINE. You tell him!

GODFREY. Don't worry, Sweet Father'll find a way to join us. He knows how long we've been awaiting his arrival. Trust me, he won't let us down.

ERNESTINE (*to audience*). But he did.

GODFREY *sits, frozen. The others dutifully clear the banquet table around him.*

GODFREY. Wait! I… I still got all of these questions I wanted to ask Sweet Father. My pockets are stuffed full of paper.

The banquet table is removed, leaving GODFREY *sitting alone.* GODFREY *pulls handfuls of paper from his pocket.* ERMINA *exits.*

But he promised and now I got to wait another year before I get the answers. Oh no! If he is the God he proclaims to be, I need his answers now, I need him to help me move on.

ERNESTINE (*to audience*). He'd followed an address on a bottle of something that soothed him and supposed that potion would be in abundance up North.

GODFREY. Back home, everything was played according to a plan. Right? I knew just how my life would be. I knew everything I needed to know. And now I got me a new pair of shoes worthy of the finest angel and a handful of misgivings.

GERTE (*comforting* GODFREY). We came together because of Sweet Father, there is power in that.

GODFREY *slowly exits.* GERTE *turns to* ERNESTINE.

(*Thinking aloud.*) But I've been to speakers' corner, there are a half-dozen messiahs waiting to replace him.

ERNESTINE (*to audience*). Not God, imagine.

Lights rise on a smirking, laughing LILY. *She stops abruptly and lights a cigarette in the shadow of the three gold balls of a pawn shop. She rips off her wristwatch and earrings.*

Lily said God was given to us by a government bent on pacifying the masses with religion. And now Gerte had gone one step further and threatened to take our God completely away.

Scene Two

Brower Park. ERMINA *stands in a pool of light.*

ERMINA (*without a breath*). Scat cat, hip, jive, cool baby, dip
dive. Bebop, shoo bop, de dap, de dop. Give me some skin,
babe. Far out, sweet daddy. Hang tight, hang loose, dig this,
out of sight, take it easy, you're blowing my mind,
everything is copacetic, the most, gonest, funky!

Lights rise on ERNESTINE.

ERNESTINE (*to audience*). Ermina is discovering the language
of the city.

ERMINA. Back off, Ernie, your vibe ain't happening.

ERNESTINE (*to audience*). Gerte has driven her to hopeless
popularity. James Watson, Simon Richards, Lawrence
Alleyne and even that Chinese fella. Victory and Virtue. The
third 'V' got lost somewhere near Trenton along with Father
Divine's Duesenberg.

ERMINA *pulls her sweater tight.*

ERMINA. Hush now, I don't want the boys to think we too
chummy.

ERNESTINE (*to audience*). It's finally green like down home.
We're supposed to be at the market, but we're in Brower
Park. All the teenagers are gathered in clusters arranged by
blocks. Near the water fountain is Bergen Street, Kingston
Avenue is huddled by the park entrance and it's just me and
Ermina from Dean, being we're the only colored people on
that block. (*To* ERMINA.) Don't run off, you hear. Ain't
supposed to be talking to no boys.

ERMINA....Oh Ernie, leave me alone, if ya wasn't so prissy
maybe a boy might give ya a smile or something. Why don't
you go off to the pictures, you're cramping my space.

ERMINA *flicks her fingers and turns up her dress. An upbeat Louis Jordan tune plays.* ERMINA *snaps her fingers to the beat.*

ERNESTINE (*to audience*). I can see the gals whispering about us, 'They communist, she father married a white lady.'

ERMINA. 'What it like living up there with a white lady?' 'She make you scrub the floors?' 'She really blonde?' 'Hear they smell like a wet dog when their hair gets wet?' 'She a Nazi like Adolph Hitler?'

ERNESTINE (*to audience*). The only reason they bother to talk to me is to ask about Gerte.

ERMINA. LEAVE US ALONE, IT AIN'T OUR FAULT SHE WHITE!

ERNESTINE *smiles. Music continues to play in the distance.*

ERNESTINE (*to audience*). Well, it's a warm day at least, perfect for a celebration. Somebody got a car radio, can listen to new, hip songs for a change.

ERMINA *approaches* ERNESTINE. *They dance together.* ERMINA *breaks away.*

ERMINA. I got me four invitations to the dance. I don't know which to choose. It so hard.

ERNESTINE. Daddy ain't gonna let you go nohow.

ERMINA. Maybe that boy over there. He father run a funeral home up on St John's.

ERNESTINE. He don't look like nothing.

ERMINA. He look like money, plenty good enough for me. (*Smiles gloriously.*)

ERNESTINE. Oh, go on, he ain't even looking over here.

ERMINA. Shucks. He looking. (*Gives a 'Lily' wave.*)

ERNESTINE. Oooo, I'm telling Daddy. He told me to watch you.

ERMINA. Watch what? Who was watching he when he run off and married he-self a white lady. Shhhhh.

ERNESTINE. What?

ERMINA. I do believe Mommy's scratching to get out of her grave. I can hear her nails breaking away at the pine. I wouldn't blame her half a bit if she started a good old-fashion haunting.

ERNESTINE. Ooooo. You taking Mommy's name in vain.

A moment.

ERMINA. I ain't listening to ya nohow.

ERNESTINE. Little Miss Sassy. What's wrong with ya?

ERMINA. Nothing. (*A moment.*) I'll tell ya something, though, if I had me twenty dollars I'd get Randall's cousin who was in prison to break you-know-who's kneecaps like they done that boy over on Park Place. That way she'd get scared and go away.

ERNESTINE. They done what?

ERMINA. See, if you didn't sit in the house on your behind all day you'd know. Whack! Whack! Yup!

ERNESTINE. Nah!

ERMINA. I hate it up here! Nothing seem like it should be. Nothing! It ain't normal for a white lady to be living in a house with colored folks. She don't even cook right.

Lights rise on the living room. GERTE stands over the table chopping cabbage. Potted plants and colorful rugs decorate the room in a feeble attempt to brighten the otherwise bleak apartment. The dressmaker's dummy prominently displays ERNESTINE's graduation dress, which is beginning to take shape. ERNESTINE pins the hem on her dress. ERMINA sits at the table, intensely watching GERTE. She studies the woman with a scientist's scrutiny.

GERTE. Such a pretty girl shouldn't wear a sour face. You must like complaining very much.

ERMINA. Maybe… Was you one of them Jew-hating Germans, them Nazis?

GERTE *stops what she is doing*. ERNESTINE *shoots* ERMINA *a cautionary glance*.

GERTE. What sort of question is that?

ERMINA. I don't know, it seem direct.

GERTE. That's ridiculous. What do you think? Who put those thoughts in your head?

ERMINA. Mrs Levy says –

GERTE. She's an old woman. You think I can bear Mrs Levy's whispering? The grinder is from the same town as my father. He married a Jewess. Mrs Levy trusts him with her finest cutlery.

ERMINA. She say –

GERTE. As long as there is rent in the envelope my business is not hers!

ERMINA. Well. (*Snatches up a magazine from the couch and heads toward the front door*.)

ERNESTINE. Where are you going?

ERMINA. I'm gonna sit on the stoop and git some fresh air. Someone's a little too persnickety.

ERMINA *flips up the back of her dress and exits*. ERNESTINE *continues to work on her dress, periodically glancing up at* GERTE. *Silence*.

GERTE. 'Persnickety', what is this word?

ERNESTINE. It mean… persnickety.

GERTE *returns to her task*.

GERTE. Ernie?

ERNESTINE. Yes, ma'am.

GERTE. Why don't you ever speak to me?

ERNESTINE. I don't know.

GERTE. It makes me uncomfortable for both of us... to be here and no one says anything. Why don't you go outside with Ermina then? (*A moment.*) Don't you have friends, Ernie?

ERNESTINE. No, ma'am.

A moment.

GERTE. What do you like to do?

ERNESTINE. I like going to the pictures.

GERTE. Me too.

ERNESTINE. I like going with Sister 'cause she always got something wise to say.

GERTE. Maybe we can go together. Your father thinks we are similar. We both like the pictures. Yes?

ERNESTINE. I don't think so.

GERTE. Why not?

ERNESTINE. The kids in school would talk.

GERTE. I see... Ah... Your dress is coming along very nicely. I was looking at the lace you bought and I think it's quite nice around the collar where the stitching is crooked.

ERNESTINE (*to audience*). Crooked? My mother could make the most perfect seams. Almost like a machine.

GERTE. If you want me to help you... well... I'm not much of a seamstress... I... (*Fumbles with the cabbage.*)

ERNESTINE (*to audience*). In the newsreels, the Germans always wore the ragged faces of our enemy.

GERTE *smiles uncomfortably.*

GERTE. Are you scared of me, Ernie?

ERNESTINE. Yes, ma'am.

GERTE. What do you think?... I'm not horrible, really.

ERNESTINE. No, ma'am.

GERTE. I'm just not used to so much silence.

> GERTE *walks over to the radio and turns it on. Swing music fills the room.*

ERNESTINE. Daddy don't like music in the house on Sunday.

GERTE. What a shame, it's a lovely radio.

> ERNESTINE *switches off the radio.*

> It is so like him to buy something he doesn't use. (*She chuckles.*)

ERNESTINE. He didn't buy it.

GERTE. When I was young there was always music in the house. My brother played the piano. My father the viola and I… I… (*A moment. She returns to chopping cabbage and accidentally nicks her finger.*) Damn!

> LILY, *hungover and in her bathrobe, enters and sits down, letting her head rest against the table.*

> Ahh! Late night. We've missed you today. How goes we?

LILY. What do you mean?

GERTE. Are you feeling well?

LILY. Copacetic. And I thought you were asking some deep German question.

GERTE. I'm glad to see you are feeling better.

> *She pours* LILY *a glass of water from a pitcher. She sets it in front of* LILY. LILY *quickly drinks down the water.*

> Would you like some coffee?

> GERTE *returns to cutting cabbage. When* ERNESTINE *isn't looking,* GERTE *periodically shoves cabbage into her mouth.* LILY *turns on the radio, flipping through the stations until she finds bebop. She does a few steps.*

LILY. Smooth. Huh?

GERTE *and* ERNESTINE *exchange glances.*

Yeah, bebop. Dig. Listen to that, he takes a melody we've heard a hundred times and makes it familiar in an entirely different way.

GERTE *stops to listen.*

GERTE. Yes. It is wonderful. I like this music very much. I used to hear this colored musician play jazz in Berlin, when I was a teenager, before the war. Have you ever heard of Pierre Boussard?

LILY. No.

GERTE. He said he was quite famous in the United States, but they all say this to German girls. (*Laughs at the memory.*) He played the saxophone beautifully. He was a colored man.

LILY. Yeah, you said that.

GERTE. When I arrived in America, I thought all colored people either played jazz or were laborers. I didn't know. I grew up in a small town about seventy kilometers from Berlin. I could tell you the name of every person, man, woman and child who lived there. Ask me and I could tell you exactly. I was seventeen – (*To* ERNESTINE.) your age, when I went to the city and first used a proper toilet. Ya. And in Berlin, I tasted tobacco and whiskey. Ya. And danced to 'insane' music, as my father called it. 'Caution abandoned.' And imagine hearing the Negro voice for the first time on a recording, oh, it was… brilliant. (*Groping for words.*) It was freeing to know that someone so far away could give a musical shape to my feelings. I wanted to visit America, see the people who create this music. Go West. The pictures. Same dreams everyone has.

ERNESTINE. Yeah?

GERTE. I thought I was as pretty as the girls in the pictures. Stupid. (*A moment. She savors the music.*) It was wonderful, at least for a while. Then it got difficult, the Nazis, the war, and things happen just as you're finding yourself.

(*A moment. She turns off the radio. To* ERNESTINE.) But Godfrey doesn't like.

Silence.

LILY. Godfrey don't like the sound of the rainfall. Godfrey don't like nothing he can't control. Don't you ever want to scratch up his shoes, crumple his hat?

GERTE *begins to laugh.*

GERTE. I like that he comes home every day at the same time with cookies in his pocket and smelling of sweets. I like that he dresses so finely to go and bake bread.

LILY. Well, I'm glad somebody does. (*Giggles as she retrieves a glass and a bottle of whiskey.*) I'm just taking a nip to make my headache go away. You want some, Gertie?

GERTE. Gerte. No thank you, I refrain out of respect for the time of day.

LILY. What are ya talking about? It's three o'clock in the afternoon, bar's been open going on three hours.

GERTE *and* ERNESTINE *watch* LILY *self-consciously wipe the glass and pour herself a generous glass of whiskey.*

What? I don't generally do this, but I've been nervous as of late.

GERTE (*sarcastically*). Just how is your... 'revolution'? Working hard? You're spending a lot of time up at the headquarters in Harlem. Where is it exactly?

LILY. Lenox Avenue.

GERTE. That's right, Lenox Avenue. I haven't heard you mention it in quite some time.

LILY *stands.*

ERNESTINE. Yeah, you ain't said much.

LILY. 'Cause it's liable to end up in one of your essays. You got too much imagination to keep a simple secret. You gotta cigarette, Gertie?

GERTE *glances over at* ERNESTINE, *then reluctantly reaches into her apron and produces a cigarette.* GERTE *returns to chopping.*

A light?

GERTE *tosses* LILY *a pack of matches.*

GERTE. Godfrey mentioned that you were searching for work? I saw a sign for an agency on Nostrand. If you want I will write down the address when I pass.

LILY. That's very helpful of you. But nobody wants to hire a smart colored woman. And I ain't gonna be nobody's maid. Too many generations have sacrificed their souls in pursuit of the perfect shine.

GERTE *busies herself with cutting again.*

GERTE. My mother used to get dressed every day, no matter whether she had someplace to go or not. Even after she fell ill she'd dress each morning as though the ritual could ward off the inevitable.

LILY. I'll note that. Anyway, my suit's in the cleaners. A nightgown, a Fifth Avenue outfit, it don't matter what I wear. The only thing people see is the brown of my skin. You hear, baby. (*Laughs.*) So why even bother to get dressed.

GERTE. Must we always do this?

LILY. What are we doing?

GERTE. Can't you forget our differences behind this closed door. When I see you I see no color. I see Lily. (*She lights a cigarette.*)

LILY. Well, when I see ya, I see a white woman, and when I look in the mirror, I see a Negro woman. All that in the confines of this here room. How about that? What do you see, Ernie? You see any differences between us?

ERNESTINE. Yeah.

LILY. There you go.

GERTE. May I say to you both, I have seen what happens when we permit our differences –

LILY (*enraged*). Don't lecture me about race. You are the last person on earth I'd look to for guidance. (*Pours another drink.*)

GERTE. You are some philosopher, you get strong after a few sips from that bottle.

LILY. What do you know?

GERTE. I nearly starved to death after the war, I know quite a bit about pain.

LILY. Oh, do you?

GERTE. Please, Lily, I don't want to have to do this…
Ernestine, darling, would you fetch me a bowl?

ERNESTINE *stands up and heads toward the kitchen.* LILY *grabs* ERNESTINE's *arm.*

LILY. You're not a servant and I didn't hear her say 'please'.

A moment.

GERTE. Please.

LILY *smiles triumphantly and releases* ERNESTINE's *arm.*

Why do you always rearrange my… my intentions?

LILY. You mean reinterpret?

GERTE. Yes.

LILY. These girls must never be made to feel like servants in their own house.

GERTE. I am their stepmother. It is from that authority that my request came. Your imagination gives me more credit than I deserve. (*Whispered.*) How long can you slip coins out of Godfrey's trousers or sell off bits of your clothing? I know how much that suit meant to you. I know, because I've sold off things of my own.

LILY (*suggestively*). Tell me this, what passes through the mind
of a man that won't even touch his wife? What's he running
from?

GERTE. We've asked each other no questions. And if his Sweet
Father does not permit us to lie as man and wife, then I
accept that. I love Godfrey.

LILY. Love, a man like him, shine his shoes more than he talks
to his own family.

GERTE. Yes... (*Laughs.*)

LILY. Well, I... know... Godfrey.

GERTE. And I know Godfrey.

  ERNESTINE *returns with the bowl*. LILY *stops herself from
  commenting*. GERTE *lifts the cabbage into the bowl*.

Did I offend you, Ernie?

ERNESTINE. No, ma'am.

GERTE (*snaps*). Don't call me 'ma'am'. It makes me
uncomfortable.

ERNESTINE. Yes, ma'am.

  GERTE *lifts the bowl and exits into the kitchen*.
  ERNESTINE *returns to working on her dress*.

LILY. She don't fool me with her throw rugs and casseroles.
She don't know the half of it. (*Impulsively flips on the radio.
She stands, holding the bottle in her hand.*) Listen to it,
Ernie, that's ours. We used to live communally in African
villages. That's the truth. And when conflict arose we'd settle
our differences through music. Each village had its own
particular timeline, a simple rhythm building outward
towards something extraordinary, like bebop. And folks
would meet at the crossroads with drums, to resolve their
problems, creating intricate riffs off of their timelines,
improvising their survival. It's a beautiful notion, ain't it? It's
more than beautiful, it's practical.

ERNESTINE (*to audience*). At least I wish she had said that, if
the past evening hadn't got the better of her senses.

Music stops abruptly and LILY *takes a drink.*

LILY. My ideas are 'premium' in some circles. (*Leans against
the dressmaker's dummy, watching* ERNESTINE *work.*)
You're fussing with that thing like it was a baby. Ain't you
got bored of it yet? (*A moment. She plops on the couch.*)
Could you get me an ashtray?

ERNESTINE (*sucking her teeth*). You need to be moving about,
been sleep all day.

LILY. Never mind what I need to be doing. I got big plans
tonight. I'm resting up. I'm not just sitting here. I'm
thinking.

ERNESTINE *finds* LILY *an ashtray, then returns to her
task; she's excited to share her work with* LILY.

ERNESTINE (*ventures*). Psst, Sister... Don't you think
Mommy would love this dress? She picked the pattern, you
know.

LILY. Why don't you tell me again.

LILY *mouths the next sentence along with* ERNESTINE:

ERNESTINE. I bet you it's gonna be the prettiest dress at
graduation... And look here, I nearly got everything right.
Except around the neck, but I've put on this lace and you
won't even notice that it's crooked. That's what Gerte says,
what do you think?

LILY. White people don't have the same flair for fashion that
we do. You give a Negro woman a few dollars, I guarantee
you, two out of three times, she'll outdress a white lady who
has store credit. Look at Gerte, she dresses like a girl without
a figure.

GERTE (*offstage*). I HEARD THAT!

LILY *giggles.*

LILY (*whispered*). Pierre Boussard.

ERNESTINE (*whispered*). You hate her, don't you?

LILY. Who?… I don't think about her enough to hate her.

GERTE *reenters with a cloth to wipe the table.* ERNESTINE *goes back to fussing with her dress.*

ERNESTINE. Sister, it might be nice to add some lace around the sleeves, so it matches.

GERTE. Lace is a lovely touch.

LILY (*without looking at the dress*). Lace makes it look prissy and, quite honestly, a little country. Gals are more sophisticated, you want something smart and to the point.

GERTE *exits into the kitchen.*

ERNESTINE (*to audience*). The lace was the finest in the Woolworth's sewing section. Expensive. We'd gone by to touch it every day after school for two weeks. Finally, Ermina was the one that stole it, that's how girls do up North.

Lights rise on ERMINA. *Her leg shakes.*

ERMINA. Mommy would really want you to have the lace. It will make the dress for sure.

ERNESTINE. So she tucked it under her sweater for me. Daddy had recently bought Gerte a pink cardigan with a satin rose and said he couldn't afford it.

ERMINA*'s leg shakes violently.*

ERMINA. Leg will stop as soon as we get home. Don't worry.

ERNESTINE. Ermina's leg shook so violently on our bus ride home I thought it was gonna come right off. We soaked it in ice and prayed. That night her leg almost fell off.

ERMINA *and* ERNESTINE. Please, Lord, forgive us for our sins, it was only this once that we transgressed, but it was for a very important cause.

ERNESTINE (*to audience*). But that next day when we looked at the lace in the light of our bedroom it was all worthwhile.

ERMINA *fades into the darkness*.

LILY. Lace is a hobby for widows and those convalescing. Frilly clothing makes you look girlish, and that's how white people like to see Negroes. They don't want to think of us as adults. So the neckline's a little crooked, that per-sona-lies it.

ERNESTINE (*wounded*). What would you have me do?

LILY. You're only gonna wear it one day in your life and then it's over. Why spend so much time sewing the lace around the neckline. It ain't like you're getting married.

ERNESTINE. How would you know?

LILY. ...All right, so maybe I don't know. Last time I wore white was to my baptism, and ask me whether I still believe in God.

ERNESTINE. Maybe you need to find that dress.

LILY *laughs*.

LILY. Ernie, I have a suit upon which I pinned many hopes. And now that suit is in the cleaners waiting for me to find the money to retrieve it. You see what I'm saying. You expecting too much from that blanched mess of fabric. What's it gonna get you?

ERNESTINE. I'm gonna graduate in it. I'll be grown.

LILY. Grown. You think 'cause you got a diploma you grown. You'll be ready to step out that door in your white dress and get a job or a husband. Only time you go out this house is if the milk is sour or to see one of them stupid picture shows.

ERNESTINE. They ain't stupid. And I'm no more afraid of walking out that door than you are to get a real job.

LILY. Really? So where you gonna go, Miss Bette? Who is gonna open their door to you? Look at you. Oh, I forgot, you'll be a wearing a white dress. With or without the 'V'?

ERNESTINE. You're the one that said that looking good is half the battle.

LILY. Did I?

ERNESTINE. I don't like the way that bottle got you talking. Why you getting on me, Sister? I worked so hard on this dress. You think that the only important thing is your uptown politics. You may have more spirit and heart than I do. But some of us don't have ideas that big. Some of us are struggling for little things, like graduating from high school.

LILY. I'm just saying it won't hurt you to get out a little more.

ERNESTINE *rips the lace off of the collar.*

ERNESTINE. There, are you happy!

LILY. The world gives nothing, Ernie. It takes.

Lights fade on LILY. ERNESTINE *stands for a moment staring at her dress.*

Scene Three

The living room. ERNESTINE *is startled as* GODFREY *and* GERTE *burst through the front door.* GODFREY*'s clothing is disheveled, his forehead is covered with blood and he holds a cloth over his eye.* GERTE*'s brightly colored dress is stained with blood.* GODFREY *takes off his spring jacket and throws it on the floor, then searches frantically for a weapon. He finds* ERNESTINE*'s sewing scissors.*

GERTE. Don't! No!

GERTE *stops* GODFREY *from going back out.*

GODFREY. I'll show those bastards! They don't know who they're messing with! I got something for them!

GERTE. GODFREY! (*Shaken and angry; to* ERNESTINE.) I told him not to speak. 'Please do not answer them, Godfrey!'

ERNESTINE. What happened?

LILY *and* ERMINA *enter.*

GODFREY. That bastard's lucky I only caught him with the side of my hand. I was outnumbered, that's all. 'Cause any other time I'd –

LILY. You'd what?

GODFREY. There we go, a colored man and a white lady trying to get from one place to another. Minding our own business –

GERTE. I must have caught their eyes –

LILY. I wonder how that happened?

GERTE. You think I asked them to speak? I forced those vulgarities out of their mouths?

GODFREY. Told 'em not to speak to my wife. 'WIFE?' Then 'nigger'.

GERTE. I did not ask them to speak!

LILY. What did you expect?

GERTE. Stupid men! You're beyond that, Godfrey. What do they know about us.

ERMINA. Who done this to you?

ERNESTINE. You hurt, Daddy!

GODFREY. Oh, they had plenty to say. Snickering and carrying on. Outnumbered. Folks on the subway nodding like it's all right for them to crack me in the face with a Coca-Cola bottle.

ERMINA *covers her ears as though trying to block out the sound.*

ERMINA (*in one breath*). Scat cat, hip, jive, cool baby, dip dive. Bebop, shoo bop, de dap, de dop. Give me some skin, babe. Far out, sweet daddy. STOP! (*She races out.*)

GODFREY (*flustered*). If... If... If... I had a... (*He paces. He inadvertently bumps into* ERNESTINE*'s dressmaker's dummy.*) Does this have to be here?

ERNESTINE. Nah, sir.

GODFREY. Then move it!

The dressmaker's dummy topples over.

LILY. Why don't you let the child alone. She ain't done this to you.

GERTE *lets out a few short cries as if gasping for air.*

ERNESTINE. You want me to get the police?

LILY. What are the police gonna do, take one look and be on their way.

GERTE. Why not get them. I'll tell them what they should do.

GODFREY. Sister's right.

LILY *tends to* GODFREY*'s eye.* GERTE *tries to take over from* LILY.

GERTE. So where are the warriors in your revolution now? Why don't they help us? How are we to lead our lives if we can't go out for a... a picture show on a Saturday night.

LILY. Welcome to our world, Miss Eva. You ain't supposed to, period! Stop! Thought you knew about all these things, being from Germany and all.

GODFREY. They messed with the wrong man! This is a thick head, been rolled half a dozen times. But I have a good mind to go back out there!

GERTE *goes to comfort* GODFREY.

GERTE. Why can't they let us alone? What did we do? We were just sitting there going to the pictures. We were just sitting there.

ERNESTINE *picks up* GODFREY*'s jacket. She reaches into the pocket and produces a handful of crumbs.*

ERNESTINE (*to* GERTE). I hate you! You did this! (*Pulls* GERTE *away from* GODFREY.) I hate you!

GODFREY. Don't say that, Darling!

GERTE *backs away from* GODFREY.

GERTE. Your head, you need some ice. I'll get. (*Exits to the kitchen.*)

LILY. Jesus, I don't want to have to explain to these children where their daddy gone. Father Divine loaded you with thoughts, but forgot to give you the consequences. These are some big issues.

ERNESTINE. She right, Daddy.

GODFREY. I didn't ask you to git in on this.

ERNESTINE. We didn't have no say to begin with.

GODFREY. Oh, you taking her side?

ERNESTINE. Nah, sir. (*Rests the jacket on the chair.*)

LILY. You see, Ernestine, that's your America. Negro sitting on his couch with blood dripping down his face. White woman unscathed and the enemy not more than five years back. You can't bring order to this world. You can't put up curtains and pot plants and have things change. You really thought you could marry a white woman and enter the kingdom of heaven, didn't ya?

GODFREY. I'm sorry I can't meet your high expectations. I'm sorry I can't uplift the race. Perhaps you should find better company.

LILY. Are you asking me to leave?

ERNESTINE. He's not asking that, Sister. Are you? No one wants you to go.

LILY. I'm asking him.

GODFREY. I will not give up my needs for yours.

LILY. What are my needs, Godfrey? They seem so basic I can't imagine you'd ever make the sacrifice.

GODFREY. Sandra left me with a half-dozen undarned socks and two gals that are practically women. Only meaning I had was to bring home jars for jam. When she died... Whatcha want from me, Lily?

LILY (*whispered*). I ain't good enough for you, Godfrey?

GODFREY. You plenty good.

LILY. Then why ain't I the one in your bed? You'd rather take blows to the head and be a nigger to some simple ass on the subway than lie with me.

A moment.

GODFREY.... You a communist. You trouble's guide.

LILY. And Miss Eva ain't?

GODFREY. We on different roads, Lily.

LILY. Where are you going?

She moves closer to GODFREY. GERTE *reenters.*

Remember back in Pensacola before –

GERTE. Are you all right, darling?

GODFREY (*to* LILY). I keep telling you, I ain't that man. You insult my wife, you insult me. All 'cause you got these big ideas about race and the world and we don't fit your picture.

ERNESTINE. Daddy, not now. You're –

GODFREY (*snaps*). And now you got my children taking up your lead.

LILY. You say that with such contempt for me. I'm getting tired of you constantly berating me with your sanctified notions. I'm sorry for what happened to you and Gerte, but I will never apologize for who I am. And every day in this

apartment you make me and the gals feel like we got to.
You'd have these children buried along with Sandra. Shucks,
I let a memory carry me this far, but even that memory done
run out of fuel. Where is my apology? GODFREY? Where is
my apology for all the wrongs done to me? (*Brushes past*
GERTE *and exits out the front door.*)

ERNESTINE. Sister! Sister!

She starts after LILY; GODFREY *catches her arm.*

Don't let her go. Daddy, you have no cause to treat Sister
that way. She... she... You gonna let her go, you know
where she's gonna go.

GODFREY. What can I do? Ernestine. (*Reluctantly takes out
his notepad.*) Gerte?

GERTE *lifts the rag from over* GODFREY's *eye.*

GERTE. I'm sorry, I don't know what to do. (*To* ERNESTINE.)
Lily need not be a barrier. She is so full of ideas, but you
must decide how you feel about me. (*Takes a deep breath.*)
And I don't see why she is here anyway? Has anyone
thought about how that makes me feel?... Well?

ERNESTINE. She's blood.

GODFREY. She's my wife's sister.

GERTE. I am your wife.

GODFREY. What? You want me to ask her to leave? You're
asking me to cast off everything that came before.

GERTE. I have.

GODFREY *jots something down on his pad.*

GODFREY. I'll make a note to speak to her later.

GERTE. STOP! You've assembled lists that run miles and
miles. There's an entire closet crowded with paper and
scribbles of things you need to know, things you want to do,
questions that must be answered. It would take three

lifetimes to get through all of it. (*She retrieves boxes of lists hidden beneath the furniture. She rips up the individual pieces of paper.*)

GODFREY. What the… the devil are you doing?

GERTE. If you'd pay attention to the world around you, you wouldn't have so many questions to ask.

GODFREY *tries to stop* GERTE; *they struggle wildly. She throws the papers into the air like a shower of confetti.* GODFREY *scrambles to retrieve the pieces of torn paper. In the midst of the struggle, they recognize the absurdity and begin to laugh as they throw the papers in air.* ERNESTINE *revels in the shower of paper.*

ERNESTINE (*to audience*). And upstairs, Mrs Levy watches television, too loud for this time of night, laughing.

Laughter fills the stage. GERTE *kisses* GODFREY's *wound.*

(*To audience.*) Showered in my father's uncertainty, no more questions unanswered.

Suddenly, blue, flickering light engulfs GODFREY *and* GERTE, *who kiss passionately, like film stars. A swell of music.*

(*To audience.*) We'd recovered my father from Divine only to lose him to passion. The kiss. The transforming kiss that could solve all of their problems. Their kiss, a movie-time solution.

GERTE. Now make a decision!

Lights fade on all but ERNESTINE, *who stares down at the fallen dressmaker's dummy. She bends to pick it up amidst the slips of paper.*

Scene Four

The living room. ERNESTINE *cleans up the remains of her father's questions.*

ERNESTINE (*reading*). 'Sweet Father, we come North with the idea that things will be better, but we end up doing much the same thing. Why does this happen? And where can I find solace?' (*Continues to retrieve slips of paper.*) 'Sweet Father, my daughter has shown a liking for the other sex and I don't know how to speak to her, can you give me some words?'

Lights rise on GODFREY *as* ERNESTINE *continues to scan the questions.*

GODFREY. Can you give me some words. Sweet Father, the... the boss keeps calling me 'the country nigger', in front of the other men. They laugh and I want so badly to say something, I want to knock 'em clear across the room, but I need this job. Sweet Father, this city confuse me, but all I know is to keep the door shut. Sweet Father, my wife's sister, she living with us and I don't know how long I'll be able to look away. Sweet Father, sometimes I think about sending my gals back home. Sweet Father, I've wed a white woman like you done, I loves her, but I don't know whether my children ever will? Do I gotta make a choice? Will you help me calm my rage?

Lights fade on GODFREY.

ERNESTINE (*reading*). 'Will you help me calm my rage?'

ERNESTINE *continues to gather the questions.* LILY *enters carrying an unopened bottle of whiskey in a paper bag.*

LILY. What happened here?

ERNESTINE....Daddy's questions.

A moment. LILY *looks around the room.*

I didn't know whether you'd come back.

LILY *finds it hard to look directly at* ERNESTINE. *She toys with the bottle in her hand.*

LILY. Well... actually, Ernie, I... I have been invited to a conference in upstate New York, Albany area. I been meaning to tell you. (*Continues to toy with the bottle.*) They want me to lecture or something like that. They've recognized that I'm an expert on the plight of the Negro woman. I've been thinking about going.

ERNESTINE. I know you got important things to do.

LILY. Chile, I got too many places to go, that's my problem. You know what I'm talking about. I don't have the luxury of settling down, too much to do!

ERNESTINE. You're lucky, Sister.

LILY. Me? Miss Bette, you're the one who's gonna be graduating in a few days. You'll finally get to wear that white dress. I can't wait to see you grab that diploma and march on down the aisle.

ERNESTINE. I'm scared, Sister.

LILY. You can't sit here waiting on the world to happen for you, picking up your father's questions. Let him clean up his own mess. (*Sets the whiskey bottle on the table.*)

ERNESTINE. May I have a taste?

LILY. Your daddy wouldn't like –

ERNESTINE. Daddy ain't here.

LILY *pours herself and* ERNESTINE *a drink.* ERNESTINE *reluctantly lifts the glass, takes a sip and cringes.* ERNESTINE *and* LILY *share a laugh.*

Mommy used to sit with us every evening. We'd get excited about what we had done during the day. Even the simple things became miraculous in the retelling... We'd laugh so much, Sister, like now... It ain't gonna be like that anymore, is it? I want to go someplace where folks don't come home sullied by anger.

LILY. Nobody likes for things to change, Miss Crump.

ERNESTINE (*ventures*). I think I'm a communist.

LILY. Why do you say that?

ERNESTINE. 'Cause don't nobody want to be my friend in
school. Can't I be part of your revolution, so folks heed
when I walk into the room?

LILY *laughs long and hard.*

LILY. Ernie, I came up here just like you, clothing so worn and
shiny folks wouldn't even give me the time of day. I came
with so much country in my bags folks got teary-eyed and
reminiscent as I'd pass. It was the year white folk had burned
out old Johnston, and we'd gathered at Reverend Duckett's
church, listening to him preach on the evils of Jim Crow for
the umpteenth time, speaking the words as though they alone
could purge the demon. He whipped us into a terrible frenzy
that wore us out. I'd like to say I caught the spirit, but
instead I spoke my mind… A few miscalculated words, not
knowing I was intended to remain silent. You know what a
miscalculation is? It's saying, 'If y'all peasy-head Negroes
ain't happy, why don't you go up to City Hall and demand
some respect. I'm tired of praying, goddamnit!' Mind ya, I
always wanted to leave. And mind ya, I might not have said
'goddamn'. But those words spoken by a poor colored gal in
a small cracker town meant you're morally corrupt. A
communist, Ernie. Whole town stared me down, nobody
would give me a word. It was finally the stares that drove me
North. Stares from folks of our very persuasion, not just the
crackers. You want to be part of my revolution? You know
what I say to that, get yourself a profession like a nurse or
something so no matter where you are or what they say, you
can always walk into a room with your head held high,
'cause you'll always be essential. Period. Stop! But you
gotta find your own 'root' to the truth. That's what I do. Was
true, is true, can be true, will be true. You ain't a communist,
Ernie!

ERNESTINE. No?

LILY. Not yet! You just thinking, chile. A movie star can't have politics.

LILY *laughs. A moment.* GERTE *enters from the bedroom, flustered.*

GERTE. Excuse me. I heard the noise. I thought Godfrey was home. Sometimes I get scared in the dark when he is at work. I fix myself something to eat and I feel better. (*Gives* ERNESTINE *an imploring smile, then heads toward the kitchen.*)

LILY. Do you want a drink?

GERTE *stops short.*

GERTE (*surprised*). Thank you.

LILY *passes her glass to* GERTE. GERTE *knocks the drink back.*

LILY. Easy does it.

GERTE *refrains from making eye contact with* LILY.

It's a little quiet, ain't it? Wouldn't mind some music.

ERNESTINE *turns on the radio. Mambo music plays.* LILY *pours* GERTE *another drink. The women stand awkwardly for a moment.* LILY *offers* GERTE *her hand.* GERTE *accepts it. The music swells as they are swathed in the brilliant, flickering glow of the cinema.* LILY *and* GERTE *do an elaborate mambo.*

ERNESTINE (*to audience*). At least I wish they had. But there they stood.

The music stops abruptly. The women stand silently, facing each other.

LILY. Are you sure you don't want a drink?

GERTE. I should go to sleep, really. (*She begins to leave.*) Good night. (*As she leaves, she touches* LILY*'s shoulder.*) I wish –

LILY. Please don't embarrass me with your articulation of regrets.

GERTE *smiles and exits.*

(*To* ERNESTINE.) You're looking a little tired yourself.

ERNESTINE. Will you turn out the light?

LILY *gives* ERNESTINE *a hug.* ERNESTINE *exits.* LILY *makes her way over to* ERNESTINE*'s graduation dress. She rips the lace off of the bottom of her slip and begins to sew it around the collar.*

Epilogue

Summer

ERNESTINE *stands in a spotlight wearing her white graduation gown, with the ragged lace border around the collar. She holds a diploma in her hand.*

ERNESTINE (*to audience*). The principal says the world is to be approached like a newborn, 'handled with care'. What he didn't say was what happens when the world doesn't care for you.

Lights rise on the living room, which is decorated for a graduation celebration. A huge white cake sits on the table.

GODFREY, GERTE *and* ERMINA. Surprise!

GODFREY. I hope you don't mind if I take that diploma down to the job with me, I want to show it off to the boys.

ERNESTINE. Just don't get anything on it.

ERMINA. Better not!

GODFREY. Look! Your favorite cake, three layers, custard filling.

ERMINA. But you gotta open the gifts before anything.

ERNESTINE *lifts one of her presents.*

GODFREY. Oooo, and I got a surprise for ya also.

GERTE. Not yet, Godfrey.

GODFREY. I can't wait... Down at the bakery they need another gal. One word from me and you're as good as in.

ERNESTINE (*to audience*). Bakery? Imagine a life in the bakery by his side with no greater expectation than for the bread to rise.

A moment. GODFREY *smiles gloriously.*

(*To* GODFREY.) I don't know that that's what I want to do.

GERTE. It's a good job, Ernie, steady.

GODFREY. I... I already told the folks at the bakery that you'd be working for them.

ERNESTINE. You should have asked me, Daddy.

GODFREY (*wounded*). I don't see what the problem is. You have no job promised and nobody's knocking down this door to ask for your hand in marriage. I'm offering you something wonderful, Ernie.

ERNESTINE *turns away from her father.*

ERNESTINE. But Daddy, I'm going to Harlem.

GODFREY. Forget about Lily, you follow her you know what you'll be taking on. Don't be this way, it's a happy day. Gerte cooked up a meal and ya got a whole room full of presents.

ERNESTINE. I ain't following Lily.

GODFREY. Then why else would you want to go?

ERNESTINE. Why are you always blaming somebody else? Maybe this doesn't have anything to do with anybody but you and me. You're always making the right choice for yourself, but you never think about how I may feel.

GODFREY. That ain't true. I came North for you gals, please, Darling –

ERNESTINE. I'm not Darling Angel, I'm Ernestine Crump, it says so on my diploma.

GODFREY. I didn't mean it that way.

ERNESTINE. But you did!

GODFREY. Look at you, Ernie. You're my little gal, you really don't know what's out there.

ERMINA. Why ya gonna go?

Lights slowly begin to fade on all but ERNESTINE.

ERNESTINE (*to audience, smiling*). Poor Ermina. She'll carry my memory in her leg now, a limp that will never quite heal.

ERMINA *limps across the room to* ERNESTINE.

The room in the basement. The mourning. The prayers. The dinner table. The television upstairs. The sweets.

GODFREY. You're old enough to make up your own mind. I fed you for years, I took up where your mother left off. If you ain't happy, you've gotten what I can give.

GERTE. Godfrey, she'll be all right.

ERMINA. Let's go outside and sit on the stoop, watch all the white gals in their graduation dresses. Let's go to a movie, forgit about all this until tomorrow. Let's go down to Coney Island and pretend to ride the Cyclone. Let's get some ice cream.

Lights continue to fade on all but ERNESTINE, *who is swathed in the blue, flickering glow of the movies.* GERTE *sings a few lines from 'Falling in Love Again'.*

GODFREY (*sing-song*). I got something in my pocket for my baby.

ERNESTINE (*to audience*). In the movies the darkness precedes everything. In the darkness, the theatre whispers with anticipation…

She stands, lost and confused on a noisy, crowded street corner in Harlem.

Finally, Harlem… Lost… (*To invisible crowd.*) Does anybody know how I get to Lenox Avenue? Lenox Avenue? The Party headquarters! You know, Lily Ann Green. Lily Ann Green. Lily… (*Holds out a sheet of paper.*) Nothing's there but an empty bar, 'Chester's'. Blue flashing neon, sorta nice. I order a sloe gin fizz and chat with the bartender about the weather. It looks like rain. It's only men. They make me nervous. But they remember Lily. Everyone does. So I tell them, 'I've come to enlist, in the revolution, of course. To fight the good

fight. I got a high-school diploma. I'll do anything. I'll scrub
floors if need be. You see, I care very much about the status
of the Negro in this country. We can't just sit idly by, right?
Lily said we used to live communally in Africa and solve our
differences through music by creating riffs off of a simple
timeline building out toward something extraordinary, like…
bebop.' The bartender tells me he knows just the place I'm
looking for, address 137th Street between Convent and
Amsterdam. And here I find myself, standing before this great
Gothic city rising out of Harlem. Black, gray stone awash. At
the corner store they tell me it's… City College. (*A moment*.)
In the movies… well… Years from now I'll ride the subway
back to Brooklyn. I'll visit Daddy and Gerte and we'll eat a
huge meal of bratwurst and sweet potatoes and realize that we
all escape somewhere and take comfort sometimes in things
we don't understand. And before I graduate, Ermina will give
birth to her first child, lovely Sandra. She'll move home with
Nana for a few years and she'll be the one to identify Lily's
cold body poked full of holes, her misery finally borne out.
Years from now I'll read the *Communist Manifesto*, *The Souls
of Black Folk* and *Black Skin, White Masks* and find my dear
Lily amongst the pages. Still years from now I'll remember
my mother and the sweet-smelling humid afternoons by the
Florida waters, and then years from now I'll ride the Freedom
Bus back down home, enraged and vigilant, years from now
I'll marry a civil servant and argue about the Vietnam War,
integration and the Black Panther movement. Years from now
I'll send off one son to college in New England and I'll lose
the other to drugs and sing loudly in the church choir. (*Lifts
her suitcase, beaming*.) But today I'm just riffing and walking
as far as these feet will take me. Walking… riffing…
riffing… riffing.

Lights slowly fade as ERNESTINE *continues to repeat the
line over and over again. A traditional version of 'Some
Enchanted Evening' plays, then gives way to a bebop version
of the song. Blackout.*

End of play.